Woke Free Work Places

Removing the Racist "Equity" Aspect of DEI

by Promoting "Merit" Based Policies & Woke Free Work Environments

By

Corey Lee Wilson

Woke Free Work Places

Woke Free Work Places: Removing the Racist "Equity" Aspect of DEI

Fratire Publishing books can be purchased in bulk with special discounts for educational purposes, organizational gifts, sales promotions, and special editions can be created to specifications. All inquiries for such can be made below.

FRATIRE PUBLISHING LLC
4533 Temescal Canyon Rd. # 308
Corona, CA 92883
www.FratirePublishing.com
FratirePublishing@att.net
(951) 638-5502

FratirePublishing
Relevant Books for **SAPIENT** Beings

Fratire Publishing is all about common sense and relevant books for sapient beings. If this sounds like you and you can never have enough common sense, wisdom and relevancy, then visit us at www.FratirePublishing.com.

Printed paperback and eBook by Ingram Spark in La Vergne, Tennessee, USA
Copyright © March 2025
ISBN 978-1-953319-47-0 (Paperback)
ISBN 978-1-953319-42-5 (eBook)
WFWP-01-PDF (pdf)
WFWP-01-EPUB (epub)
LCCN 2025902124

Book cover logo by dasignlady at:
https://www.redbubble.com/people/dasignlady/shop?artistUserName=dasignlady&iaCode=
all-stickers.

Woke Free Work Places

Contents

Acknowledgements

Below are the major contributors to *Woke Free Work Places: Removing the Racist "Equity" Aspect of DEI* that were borrowed from, verbatim, quoted, and conceptualized, from a little to a lot. Wherever this happened, their contributions and sources are acknowledged in the Resources section at the end of the book, as well as the Index section, and done intentionally so as to not distract the reader from the themes and messages covered throughout the chapters of the handbook.

Christopher F. Rufo – Is an American conservative activist, contributing editor of *City Journal,* New College of Florida board member, senior fellow at the Manhattan Institute for Policy Research, and leading the fight against Progressivism madness in American institutions. He is a vocal opponent of critical race theory, former documentary filmmaker and fellow at the Discovery Institute, the Claremont Institute, The Heritage Foundation, and the Foundation Against Intolerance and Racism. In 2022, he earned a Master of Liberal Arts in Extension Studies from Harvard Extension School.

City Journal – Is a public policy magazine and website, published by the Manhattan Institute for Policy Research, that covers a range of topics on urban affairs, such as policing, education, housing, and other issues. The *City Journal* and its authors were the most widely used resource for *Woke Free Work Places.*

S.A.P.I.E.N.T. Being – The Society Advancing Personal Intelligence and Enlightenment Now Together (S.A.P.I.E.N.T.) Being is the leading anti-woke and anti-progressivism madness organization and think tank in the USA. They publish *Progressivism Madness: A SAPIENT Being's Guide to the Idiocracy and Hypocrisy of the 'Regressivism' Movement*, a textbook from their Sapient Conservative Textbook (SCT) Program, an alternative social studies textbooks program to counter woke and progressive madness in America's educational institutions, and help return conservative values, viewpoint diversity, and sapience to high school and college campuses.

An Introduction to Diversity, Equity, Inclusion and Wokeness

With rapidity and stealth, the diversity, equity and inclusion (DEI) ideology has come to replace the classical liberal values of merit, excellence, and intelligence (MEI).

The time for a national debate over the conflicting values of DEI and MEI is long overdue in the academy, professional organizations, media, government and large technology companies. DEI bureaucracies have mushroomed and many operate behind the scenes with ambiguous DEI definitions, goals and policies.

Drawing upon many of the points in the Robert Maranto, Michael Mills and Catherine Salmon article "What do we really mean by 'diversity, equity and inclusion'?" published in *The Hill* in November 2024:

This is a significant cultural and ideological revolution, one that has been accomplished with almost no debate or operationalization of terminology. The unexamined acceptance of DEI, however defined, is surprising in a free society where critics are encouraged to challenge and debate significant social changes.

At the S.A.P.I.E.N.T. Being, America's leading anti-wokeness organization and non-profit think tank, the time for a national debate over the conflicting values of DEI and MEI is long overdue.

As noted in *The Hill* article: Who originated DEI? Why DEI and not another set of laudable values? Does "equity" refer to opportunity or result? How do those of mixed race fit in diversity assessments? Is the goal of racial representation proportionate to that of the population, the history of marginalization, or something else? DEI terms are defined so obtusely that they can refer to a spectrum of policies from mere platitudes to radical agendas including litmus tests and racial quotas.

In its most radical forms, DEI is derivative of neo-Marxist identitarian ideologies that attribute virtually all average group differences—from arrest rates to medical school admissions—to systemic discrimination. However, average group differences in outcomes can reflect a variety of factors (see Jared Diamond's "Guns, Germs and Steel"). The unexamined acceptance of DEI, however defined, is surprising in a free society where critics are encouraged to challenge and debate significant social changes.

For example, one-fifth of the advertisements for higher education faculty jobs (and more for prestigious posts) require applicants to write statements of allegiance to DEI. Academic employment often depends on DEI relevant presentations at scholarly conferences and publications in scholarly journals. Increasingly, scholars are required to explain in advance how their research supports DEI. Such litmus tests are traditionally associated with totalitarian regimes, and in America, with McCarthyism.

We all know how well those turned out.

Professional organizations such as the American Psychological Association, the American Bar Association, and even the more moderate American Political Science Association are adopting DEI initiatives, embracing empirically contested concepts such as implicit bias and endorsing legally questionable hiring and admissions policies that utilize de facto racial quotas.

In the academy, DEI and other identitarian orthodoxies are often mandated to be taught in student orientations and required courses, and enforced by campus DEI bureaucrats who now outnumber history faculty. By categorizing virtually any criticism as "prejudiced," DEI bureaucracies can chill free speech and have empowered some college presidents to slander their critics as bigots and then terminate them. Program renewals for academic departments, and thus continued employment for professors and graduate students, are increasingly tied to embracing DEI rhetoric and goals.

DEI in many respects is a revolutionary ideology. But it was winning. This is in part due to fear of ostracism, censorship or termination—but also because you can't beat something with nothing.

Enter University of Chicago Professor Dorian Abbot's DEI alternative, merit, fairness, and equality (MFE), which is consistent with traditional Enlightenment and scientific values. Under MFE, academic decisions are based primarily on academic merit, well validated standardized test scores, grades and, for faculty, publication and teaching records. Individuals are primarily evaluated on their achievements, not by their group identities. This respects individual dignity and promotes the primary mission of research in higher education: the production of knowledge.

MFE also accords with public opinion. The Pew Research Center found that more than 90 percent of Americans want high school grades to influence college admissions and more than 80 percent want standardized testing to play a role. Seventy-five percent of Americans believe that gender, race or ethnicity should not factor into educational admissions decisions.

As Kenny Xu points out in "An Inconvenient Minority: The Attack on Asian American Excellence and the Fight for Meritocracy," MFE would actually increase demographic diversity by ending the unfair quotas against Asians at elite schools. One study found that at Harvard an Asian American applicant with a 25 percent chance of admission would have a 35 percent chance of admission if Caucasian, a 75 percent chance if Hispanic, and 95 percent if Black.

But the powerful avoid debating their critics. Just as Alabama segregationist governor George Wallace never debated Martin Luther King, DEI backers with institutional power show no enthusiasm for defending their ideas in real debates. Without vigorous open and civil debate, DEI bureaucracies will continue to impose doctrinal training programs, litmus tests, censorship and discrimination. Unless this is challenged, we risk entering a new era of institutionalized McCarthyism.

At the S.A.P.I.E.N.T. Being, we love diversity and inclusion in the diversity, equity, and inclusion (DEI) trilogy, and strongly support them. However, the equity part, as in equitable outcomes, is the opposite of equality, as in equality of opportunities.

Unfortunately, most Americans are not aware of the fundamental difference, which is in fact reverse racism, and if they did, they would strongly oppose it. A more appropriate and alternate approach to DEI would be merit based as Elon Musk puts it, "The point was to end discrimination, not replace it with different discrimination."

On the other hand, merit based policies work hand in hand with equality of opportunity, which the United States exemplifies and excels at.

Being the world's number one destination for immigrants, and the world's most successful multi-racial society, America is founded on the principle of equal opportunity and not the neo-Marxist and reverse racism aspect of enforcing equality of outcomes, the redistribution of wealth, power and resources based on race, religion and ideology—the illiberal "equity" portion of DEI.

1 – The False Narratives & Illiberalism of Wokeness

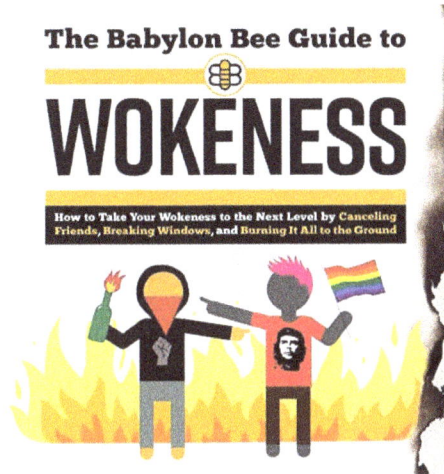

Credit: Babylon Bee.

Being "woke" is, according to Merriam-Webster, "aware and actively attentive to important facts and issues (especially issues of racial and social justice)."

The Oxford English Dictionary, which added *woke* in 2017, says the term and its derivatives are commonly used to describe people who are "alert to racial or social discrimination and injustice."

The S.A.P.I.E.N.T. Being defines *illiberalism* as a 21st century term used to describe an attitude that is close-minded, intolerant, and bigoted.

Per the Jennifer Graham. "America's 'Great Awokening,' Explained" *Desert News* March 2021 article:

Originally slang used by Black Americans, the word became part of the national lexicon in the past few years. But its meaning has already changed, and there is a divide in how the word is perceived, a divide that is both political and generational.

"OK boomer," one person responded to Musk's tweet. Born in 1971, Elon Musk isn't a baby boomer, but the tweet revealed the perception that it's older, conservative Americans who are obsessed with wokeness and its societal effects.

America's 'Great Awokening,' Explained

Politically, wokeness has been seen by some progressives and liberals as aspirational, and the hashtag #staywoke abounds on social media. Many conservatives, however, view the meaning of wokeness as a joke, or conversely, as a societal evil akin to cancel culture. They frequently use the term "woke mob" to describe collective outrage that results in a loss of professional or social standing because of a person's beliefs, statements or actions.

The political divide is not surprising, since it is Democrats and young people who are most likely to be involved in protests for racial equality, according to Pew Research Center.

But Musk, Republican Sens. Tom Cotton, of Arkansas, and Ted Cruz, of Texas, and others who use the word regularly should be aware that, almost as quickly as it came on the stage, the word's meaning has changed, according to University of Pennsylvania linguist Nicole Holliday. Here's how the word came into the American lexicon, and what it means now.

Rise of the Woke

One of the earliest uses of "woke," outside of its most common meaning (to literally wake up from sleep), was in 1962, when a glossary of African American slang defined the word as "well informed" and "up-to-date," according to Holliday, assistant professor of linguistics at the University of Pennsylvania in Philadelphia, writing for the Oxford Dictionaries blog.

Later, Holliday said, the word "woke" became mainstream in the outrage over the killing of Trayvon Martin, the 17-year-old shot by a neighborhood watchman in Florida in 2012, and the subsequent rise of the Black Lives Matter movement. But then, as more people began to use it and the word entered the mainstream political landscape, the meaning of woke was separated of its original context—wakefulness among Black Americans— and by 2016, when MTV pronounced it a "word to use," it was simply defined as "being aware—specifically in reference to current events and cultural issues."

The word changed again, as some people started using it to mock people and beliefs they disagree with, and the word is now predominantly a negative term, she said in an interview.

"This process of acquiring a pejorative meaning happened really quickly," she added. "This is something that the internet does to words. It moves them really quickly."

The evolution of woke, therefore, isn't unusual. And it's not just conservatives on Twitter (now X) who are responsible for the changing meaning. So before you use the word 'woke,' learn how its meaning has changed in the past few years.

Beyond Woke—a Return to Lincoln?

The contemporary movement known as wokeism is only the latest in a series of idealistic efforts to redeem corrupt privilege and transform human nature by means of group solidarity as explained by the Michael Knox Beran "Beyond Woke—a Return to Lincoln?" *City Journal* article in July 2022.

Much as Jacobin leaders in the French Revolution and Marxist thinkers in the nineteenth and twentieth centuries looked to the virtue and ethical purity of oppressed groups (common people, peasants, proletarian workers) to overthrow oppressing classes (the aristocracy and the bourgeoisie), so woke reformers today look to minorities and to those marginalized because of their sexual desires or gender identities to create a peaceable kingdom of intersectional harmony, in which white and cis-hetero-male groups will be stripped of their privilege and made conscious of their sins.

Yet wokeism's relentless focus on group identity runs counter to American traditions of liberty that, in Abraham Lincoln's words, reject a politics of "classification" and "caste." America, to be sure, has often failed to live up to its universalist ideals: that was the point of Lincoln's presidency. But the basic idea is that rules apply equally to everyone and should not, as F. A. Hayek wrote in The Constitution of Liberty, "single out any specific persons or group of persons" for special treatment on account of some abstract virtue, failing, or grievance that supposedly distinguishes the person or group from the rest of the citizenry.

Hayek spoke for the classical tradition of liberty, a creed that, while imperfect, remains the foundation of the American system and underlies many of its virtues. Yet it is no longer much taught in American schools. The authors of a new model for K-12 social studies aim to change this with a new educational model reminds us that classical liberalism produces better outcomes.

Correcting the Distortions of School Curricula

"We believe," the authors of American Birthright write, that "American students should comprehend aspects of American government such as the rule of law, the Bill of Rights, elections, elected office, checks and balances, equality under the law, trial by jury, grand juries, civil rights, and miliary service."

They want to correct the distortions of school curricula that "too frequently omit crucial figures" in the American story, such as George Washington, and "excise entire concepts, such as liberty or republican virtue."

It's not partisan special pleading. The orientation of the Civics Alliance, the coalition sponsoring American Birthright, is conservative, but a progressive critic would be hard put to find its program reactionary. Hayek figures in American Birthright, as does Milton Friedman. But so, too, do Karl Marx and John Maynard Keynes. Washington and Thomas Jefferson are part of the program, as are Frederick Douglass, W. E. B. Du Bois, Martin Luther King, Jr., and Malcolm X.

Far from being narrow, American Birthright would expose students to a range of human possibility. It emphasizes primary texts that young people can evaluate for themselves: the Epic of Gilgamesh, Exodus, the First Sermon of Buddha, the Analects of Confucius, the Hadith of Gabriel, the Communist Manifesto, the Port Huron Statement, and *Roe v. Wade* ruling figure alongside The Wealth of Nations and the Federalist Papers.

True, if identity politics triumph, the classical liberalism that American Birthright would resurrect will be as much a curiosity as Zoroastrianism.

But the Civics Alliance may be right in betting on the continued vitality of Lincoln-style liberalism.

Why Wokeism is Likely to Fail

Wokeism is likely to fail precisely because it borrows so copiously from earlier failed experiments in collectivist solidarity. Robespierre's ruinous republic of virtue was toppled in less than a decade, and the workers' paradises inspired by Marx have (with a few unsavory exceptions) met similar fates.

Wokeism is running up against the obstacle that doomed its predecessors: human nature. Marx, Edmund Wilson wrote, was startled to discover that the proletarian worker, given the chance, was less interested in "improving humanity" in the abstract than in joining the bourgeoisie to better his own lot. It was not "what Marx expected him to do."

If polls show Democrats losing ground with blacks, Hispanics, and Asians, it's because many of these Americans are less interested in "renegotiating the social contract" in the name of an ambiguous equity than in achieving old-fashioned American success—the prosperity that collectivist regimes conspicuously fail to deliver. Those running away from wokeism instinctively sympathize with Lincoln's classical liberal rejection of a politics of resentment that leads to lower standards of living: "Let not him who is houseless pull down the house of another, but let him work diligently and build one for himself, thus by example assuring that his own shall be safe from violence when built."

The same disjunction between utopianism and human nature is evident in wokeism's esoteric terminology, the work of intellectuals who live primarily in books and ideas. Just as those whom Robespierre and Marx sought to lift up had little interest in dialectical materialism or the dictatorship of virtue, few Americans are inspired by the woke newspeak vocabulary, the invention, James Carville said, of "people in faculty lounges in fancy colleges" who use a "different language than ordinary people. . . . They come up with a word like 'Latinx' that no one else uses. Or they use a phrase like 'communities of color.' I don't know anyone who speaks like that."

By contrast, Martin Luther King Jr.'s classically liberal language, his "dream deeply rooted in the American dream"—the dream that "all men are created equal"—continues to stir Americans regardless of group affinity. In his charity, King saw that good and evil are evenly distributed across human groups. By abandoning King's 1963 dream, wokeism reproduces the bigotry he deplored in a different key.

Wokeness: An Evil of Our Age

To truly understand everything harmful with wokeness, Victor Davis Hanson's analysis "Wokeness: An Evil of Our Age" published by the Independent Institute in September 2021 starts with the idea that "wokeness" is an ideology divorced from reality.

Nearly all of its premises are complete distortions. For example, between 2017 and 2020, minorities had made the greatest gains in employment in U.S. history. Women currently represent about 60 percent of all college students.

Recent wage gains for minority middle-class Americans outpaced those of the white working- and middle class. The latter were underrepresented in college enrollments and as graduates—but vastly overrepresented (at twice their percentage of the general population) in the toll of combat dead in Afghanistan and Iraq. Asian-Americans and a dozen other ethnic groups outpace so-called whites in per capita and household income. "White privilege" is usually a sloppy term that applies mostly to the white elites who use it to smear others.

America was in our sixth decade of "affirmative action," the euphemism of ensuring equity of result by calibrating race and gender—but not class—in hiring and admissions. Proportional representation and disparate impact continued or were even enhanced. But they became increasingly selective as entire fields from the Postal Service to professional sports were somehow exempt from racial set-asides applied to others. Quotas disappeared when the marginalized were "overrepresented" in a field.

The historical reparatory effort of the massive programs born out of the Great Society continued to address the baleful legacy of slavery that had ended over 150 years ago, as well as Southern Jim Crow laws that had largely disappeared 40-50 years ago, and the fumes of such racial toxicity. So, Martin Luther King's "content of our character" rather than the "color of our skin" was still embraced as the melting-pot ideal of the Civil Rights movement that had fought for integration and full assimilation into American society. Meanwhile, intermarriage has never been more common.

Wokeness Mythology

The desperate Left had therefore been forced to invent adjectives and phraseology like "systemic racism" and "microaggression" and "whiteness" given the vast majority of Americans did not feel or express or act out on "racism."

In other words, wokeness created the mythology that the nonwhite were worse off than ever before—a typical revolutionary fabrication to evoke the sort of hysteria necessary for an otherwise unpopular agenda. But then again, we live in an age where we were assured Hunter Biden's lost laptop was "Russian disinformation," the Steele dossier was iron-clad proof of something, and a pangolin or a bat birthed COVID-19.

The wrongful death of George Floyd in police custody—despite his later angelic deification, Floyd was in fact a felon with a history of violence toward women, arrested in the act of passing counterfeit U.S. currency—was the work of a cruel rogue cop and his incompetent enablers. Otherwise, data and statistics did not show that African American males were dying while in police custody in numbers greater than their proportions of those yearly arrested. Nor were they the victims of some pandemic of interracial hate crimes. Indeed, blacks statistically were more likely to commit rare violent interracial crimes than were others, including targeted hate crimes against other ethnic and racial groups.

Elite-Driven

Another great lie was the propaganda that the woke movement was a grass-roots movement. Yet statue-toppling, vandalism, Trotskyism, and cancel culture remain largely the work of college students, upper-middle class white coastal elites, celebrities, and privileged minorities in the media, academia, law, the corporate world, entertainment, and professional sports.

In a reductionist sense, much of the woke movement became a battle among elites to leverage diversity czars in universities, reparational quotas in administrative hiring and college admissions, and a sort of racialized intramural reseating among first-class passengers on the corporate and government Lido deck.

While wokeists harangued New York and Hollywood for more nonwhites in TV commercials, thousands of young African American males continued to be slaughtered in the inner-cities, as schools in those places resisted reform and remained indifferent to the poor quality of education offered residents. Because the culpable municipal officials—hard-Left diversity mayors, neo-Marxist district attorneys, and "reformist" police chiefs—were themselves woke, no one cared about derelict governance. And so, the killing continues unabated, surrealistically unremarked upon by the wokest.

Class considerations were suppressed, given that the beneficiaries of wokeness were not necessarily previously poor and oppressed. In our racialized madness, billionaires like LeBron James, Oprah Winfrey, Jay-Z, and Beyonce, multimillionaires like the Obamas and Colin Kaepernick, and moneyed political, corporate, entertainment, military, and sports grandees—play-acted oppression and victimization from their villas and privileged perches, in perfect Marie Antoinette fashion. All they lacked was fake peasant garb and a village at Versailles.

The architects themselves of wokeness mostly cashed in on the supposedly toxic capitalist system that they had so harangued as the ground zero of "systemic racism." So, BLM cofounder and self-described "cultural Marxist" Patrisse Cullors is now "retired"—and the savvy owner of four new homes, residing in nearly all-white tony Topanga Canyon, with a new $35,000 security gate. How else could she best use her black privilege to direct her multimillion-dollar war against "white privilege"?

Professor Ibram X. Kendi (neé Henry Rogers), whose "antiracist" new industry calls for racism to stop racism and discrimination to end discrimination, now charges his corporate and university clients a reportedly $20,000 penance fee for a phoned-in Zoom chat. (He apparently has no discount rate for the poorer of his clients). Kendi no doubt took Lenin to heart ("Capitalists will sell us the rope to hang them with.") when he hawks his video indulgences at $333 a minute.

The cultural revolutionary Ta-Nehisi Paul Coates was customarily already one step ahead and has moved on from the woke movement to a multimillion-dollar career writing black-themed comic books or adapting them to the big screen. Barack and Michelle Obama, long ago known for their cinematic creativity, leveraged a $50 million "consulting" movie deal with Netflix, whose founder is best known in California for his efforts to fund the campaign against Larry Elder, including commercials starring . . . Barack Obama.

Racist

Wokeness took the Obama-era mantra of diversity and simply shed any pretense that it was not racist. Remember, after 2009 our elites institutionalized the new-old idea that anyone claiming not to be white was suddenly part of a new inclusive oppressed class, one at war with the racial oppressors.

"Diversity" was a clever update of the previously failed Jesse Jackson idea of a victimized rainbow coalition that would aggregate, and force-multiply collective grievances against white male victimizers.

Suddenly, ethnic groups with higher per capita incomes than so-called whites were victims. There were no requisites to being "diverse" other than claiming nonwhite status. Wealthy Punjabi immigrants, Chilean aristocrats, illegal aliens fleeing racist Mexico, Nigerian doctors—anyone rich or poor, resident or citizen, victimized or not—was presto! "diverse" and thereby eligible for reparatory claims in hiring and admissions.

Many liberal whites wished to get in on it and got caught at it—whether Ward Churchill with this entire Native American tribal garb, or, on the cheaper side, Elizabeth Warren with her "high" cheek bones or racial fabulists Rachel Dolezal and Shaun King. After all, if gender is "constructed," then naturally race, too, could become a construct.

All this is dangerous because we are now logically headed to DNA-categorized ID badges reminiscent of yellow Star of David patches. Here once again Elizabeth Warren had been in the lead—claiming that her boomeranged DNA results showing a tiny drop of Native American lineage were thus proof that she was an indigenous victim after all—and so in her troubled mind truly had been deserving as the first Native American law professor at Harvard. Given this nonsense, one would think a distracted

America has no real debt and is in possession of a secure border, a thriving economy, a brilliantly educated youth, and only friends abroad.

Why is Wokeism Deadly?

Wokeism is a lethal distraction. As General Mark Milley, Defense Secretary Lloyd Austin, and Chief of Naval Operations Michael Gilday lectured the nation on the various nefarious strains of white rage, whiteness, and white supremacy, the Taliban was systematically gobbling up Afghanistan. Meanwhile their boss in the White House quoted his woke military experts in order to lie there was no danger of a general collapse. No general objected. Apparently, Biden even phoned the Afghan president in a sordid attempt to leverage him likewise to lie that all was well. The ubiquitous Alexander Vindman was not listening in this time around.

In a traditional Islamic society, what were woke Americans doing bragging about gender studies programs at an Afghan university, flying pride flags at the U.S. embassy, and encouraging honorific George Floyd street murals? All that is usually the haughty cultural imperialism of would-be winners, not the virtue signaling of a defeated and humiliated diplomatic and military cohort fleeing toward the exits.

Think of this for a second: as the U.S. bureaucracy invested trillions in Afghanistan to virtue-signal against supposed George-Floyd type racism, its media appendages said nothing back home as the black candidate for the California governorship was the target of an egg-throwing woman wearing a gorilla mask. What a grotesque reminder that empires flounder abroad as they rot at home.

So these distractions never sleep, even amid the greatest defeat and loss of global deterrence in U.S. military history since Vietnam. True ideologues that they are, even our defeated on the battlefield are unfazed in their wokeist creed.

As Kabul suffered its end of days, our bemedaled wokists were still lecturing the country about the gender ratios of the Afghan refugees on U.S. flights out, the culturally sensitive food awaiting them, and a new idea of a soft Taliban—or the notion that the medieval gangsters who had defeated the Pentagon were not really all that bad, but more likely "partners" in a shared agenda of seeing us skedaddle by August 31. Will they say that in six months?

Woke Indemnity Blinds Us to Racism and Classism

Gavin Newsom, of French Laundry repute, is the epitome of a white-male mediocrity leveraging his rich family friends to elevate himself by quid pro quo favoritism. Joe Biden has voiced the most racist rants of any presidential candidate or president in the last 50 years (just recently he referred to his own senior black official as "boy"). Both bought woke insurance that inoculates them against their hypocrisy—or perhaps further fuels their own class and racial biases with an efficacy rate much more impressive than COVID vaccinations.

The creation of the blanket term "whiteness" is racist to the core. It imputes to anyone considered not sufficiently pigmented some sort of conspiratorial evil, regardless of individual character, beliefs, family history, or ideological outlook. It is incoherent since it blames the United States, and everything in it, for whiteness, and then demands that the nonwhite south of the equator from Africa to Asia be given instant access to this supposedly failed white contaminated miasma. Scarier still for the wokist, whiteness is just the new face of the old racist "blackness," in which racists imputed to individual blacks supposedly collective pathologies in order to justify discrimination against a single individual.

Once the neo-Confederate idea of color triumphs, then there is no logical reason why "blackness," "brownness," "yellowness," "redness" and every sort of pigmentary category should not be used to condemn individuals for their supposed membership in a taboo racial tribe, massaged and negatively stereotyped for contemporary advantage. We are headed back to 1840 not ahead to 2040.

If Something Can't Go On Forever, It Will Stop

Finally, wokeism is unsustainable. We are already seeing large numbers of the supposedly "nonwhite" pushback against the wokeist trajectory, knowing that such a racialist monster may soon devour them, too. Drawing artificial racial Mason-Dixon lines inside millions of multiracial families, after the initial grifting subsides, will only incur anger at those who drew them. When Confederates embraced the one-drop, one-sixteenth rule, there was unanimous later agreement that it was not just abjectly racist, but lunatic; when the woke borrow such racial distillery it too will eventually be rejected as the crackpot hatred that it is.

There are probably some 100 million white males of the lower- and middle classes. Most feel little if any identity with the woke upper-middle class and wealthy bicoastal white male elite of some 20-30 million. If anything, a trucker from Boise has more in common with a Mexican-American sheriff in Modesto than he does with a woke techie in Menlo Park.

So, what is truly evil is the current woke trademark of loud privileged whites who scapegoat the losers in the globalist game as racist (or in the Obama-Hillary Clinton-Biden patois of "clingers," "deplorables," "irredeemables," "dregs," "chumps"), mostly out of elite condescension, virtue-signaling guilt, and pathetic contextualizing their own privilege by projecting their unearned status onto supposedly distant cultural losers.

There will be a substantial political correction to the madness, mostly because without one there is no longer a confident America abroad that advances and protects the interest of a free world challenged by nightmarish Chinese Communism.

Such racist selectivity would destroy a meritocratic and productive free market economy at home that fuels the Left's massive government redistribution.

The victory of woke would guarantee that as Americans went full pre-modern and pre-civilizational, we would look in the mirror, straining to redefine and recategorize ourselves, and then search out which particular tribal band offers us the best protection from the roving mobs—and each other.

Even the Chinese apparat could not invent a more evil, more macabre way to destroy the United States.

2 – Diversity, Equity & Inclusion Bureaucracies Are Being Exposed

UVA'S HIGHEST PAID DEI STAFF

NAME	TITLE	PAY	EST. TAXPAYER COST PAY + BENEFITS
MARTIN N. DAVIDSON	Senior Associate Dean & Global Chief Diversity Officer	$451,800	$587,340
KEVIN G. McDONALD	VP For DEI & Community Partnerships	$401,465	$521,905
TRACY M. DOWNS	Chief Diversity & Community Engagement Officer & Prof. of Urology	$312,000	$405,600
MARK STEVEN CARTWRIGHT	Senior Dir. of Procurement & Supplier Diversity Services	$224,375	$291,688
MEARA M. HABASHI	Associate Dean For DEI School of Engineering & Applied Science	$212,749	$276,574
KEISHA JOHN	Associate Dean For Diversity & Inclusion	$202,674	$268,476
RACHEL SPRAKER	Asst. VP For Equity & Inclusive Excellence	$186,800	$242,840
CHRISTIE JULIEN	Senior Asst. Dean, DEI	$177,700	$231,010
KIERAH BARNES	Dir. of Advanced Practice Diversity & Development	$172,000	$223,600
MARK CHRISTOPHER JEFFERSON	Asst. Dean for Community Engagement & Equity	$166,260	$216,138

Source: UVA FOIA

☑ LEARN MORE AT OPENTHEBOOKS.COM

Credit: Adam Andrzejewski, CEO/Founder of OpenTheBooks.com.
University of Virginia (UVA) highest paid DEI staff.

DEI course mandates at public universities cost taxpayers nearly $2 billion, shocking report from Steven McGuire, "How One College Spends More Than $30M on 241 DEI Staffers ... and the Damage it Does to Kids" published in the *New York Post* in January 2024 reveals:

One day after winning the national college football championship, the University of Michigan was recognized as a leading competitor in another popular collegiate sport: wasteful diversity, equity and inclusion spending.

Having recently embarked on a new five-year DEI plan, UM is paying more than $30 million to 241 DEI staffers this academic year alone, Mark Perry found in a recent analysis for the College Fix.

That represents an astounding expansion of the school's already-infamous DEI bureaucracy, which had a mere 142 employees last year. And the price tag accounts for neither the money spent on programming and office expenses nor the hundreds of other employees who use some of their time to assist with DEI initiatives.

How One College Spends More Than $30M on 241 DEI Staffers … and the Damage it Does to Kids

These expenditures are a reckless waste of taxpayer money considering the impact of UM's last five-year plan. It cost $85 million, and what did it accomplish asks McGuire?

According to the university's Black Student Union, "85 million dollars was spent on DEI efforts and yet, Black students' experience on campus has hardly improved." Hispanic and Asian enrollments increased, but black enrollment dropped slightly from 4.3% in 2016 to 3.9% in 2021.

And the *Chronicle of Higher Education* reports, "The percentage of students who were satisfied with the overall campus climate decreased from 72 percent in 2016 to 61 percent in 2021."

These results are consistent with findings at other institutions.

A Claremont Institute study of Texas A&M University found that despite an annual DEI budget of $11 million, the percentage of students who felt they belonged at the school dropped significantly from 2015 to 2020: Among whites, the number went from 92% to 82%; among Hispanics, from 88% to 76%.

Among blacks, there was an astonishing drop from 82% to 55%.

At the University of California, Berkeley, whose Division of Equity and Inclusion boasts 152 staffers and a $36 million budget, black undergraduate enrollment dropped from 3% in 2010 to 2% in 2021.

The truth is that DEI does not work and frequently makes matters worse.

DEI trainings not only fail to achieve their purposes but often exacerbate grievances and divisions by antagonizing people and teaching them to monitor one another for microaggressions and implicit biases.

DEI often leads to illegal activities, too.

The University of Washington recently revealed, for example, that its psychology department actively discriminated against faculty candidates based on race, elevating a lower-ranked candidate for a position over others because of a desire to hire a black scholar.

In another case, a former assistant director of multicultural student services (MSS) at the University of Wisconsin-Eau Claire recently filed a lawsuit alleging that despite exemplary performance reviews, she was harassed and discriminated against simply for being white, until she resigned.

"We don't want white people in the MSS office," a student reportedly said during an open house. Even with the failures and the excesses, Michigan is not the only school ramping up its DEI expenditures:

- Another College Fix analysis found that Ohio taxpayers are spending $20.38 million annually on DEI salaries and benefits at UM's famous rival, Ohio State University, where the number of DEI bureaucrats has grown from 88 in 2018 to 189 in 2023.

- Oklahoma's public universities spent $83.4 million on DEI over the last 10 years.

- Florida's public universities reported spending $34.5 million during the 2022-23 academic year.

- The University of Wisconsin was poised to spend $32 million over the next two years.

Why not use all that money to give students a much-needed tuition break? Or why not fund need-based scholarships for promising students instead of giving cash to bureaucrats who are actively damaging our higher education institutions?

Fortunately, some states are taking action.

Florida and Texas passed laws eliminating DEI bureaucracies, and Wisconsin lawmakers recently curbed DEI in the state university system by compelling the board of regents to agree to DEI staff cuts and a hiring freeze.

Many other state systems have ended the use of DEI statements in hiring, recognizing they are used to screen out heterodox thinkers when studies show ideological diversity is beneficial to the search for knowledge, which is a university's core purpose.

And that points to the greatest cost of DEI: While the financial waste is appalling, the price of expecting everyone on campus to conform to an ideology that undermines free expression and excludes intellectual diversity, two foundational values of the academy, is one we should be unwilling to pay.

How Discriminatory DEI Ideology Replicates Itself in the Federal Bureaucracy

If you're like most Americans, you've heard the acronym "DEI." You may also know that it stands for "diversity, equity, and inclusion." What you may not know is that those words are as accurate as the word "Democratic" in the "Democratic People's Republic of Korea" (today's North Korea) or the "German Democratic Republic" (the former East Germany) explains Simon Hankinson's "How Discriminatory DEI Ideology Replicates Itself in the Federal Bureaucracy" report by The Heritage Foundation in October 2023.

Creating Disparity From the Idea of Equality

DEI is, in fact, a reductionist ideology that sees all disparities of performance as evidence of racism. It promotes discrimination based on immutable characteristics like skin color, and prizes equal outcomes over equal opportunity.

The efficiency and credibility of the U.S. State Department, military, and federal bureaucracy are being undermined by the Biden administration's relentless insertion of DEI into every facet of operations, not least personnel.

As the *Wall Street Journal's* Jason Riley writes, "the progressive left's response" to gaps between racial groups in performance outcomes "has been to wage war on meritocracy rather than focus on improving instruction" in K-12 schools, where lie the roots of group disparities that show up years later.

Discrimination in Incarceration

The woke creed of applying present discrimination to make up for past discrimination now infects everything from helping the homeless to criminal justice. California may soon pass a law that "requires judges to consider a convicted criminal's race when determining prison sentences," to "rectify the historical racial bias deeply ingrained in the criminal justice system." Some activists even suggest that victims of crime should be treated differently based on their race.

DEI as practiced in most American organizations is antithetical to America's fundamental values and often illegal. And yet, DEI bureaucracies are now well entrenched across academia and government.

Hiring Practices

Most American universities are dominated by Leftist ideology. Viewpoint diversity is vanishing, to the detriment of both faculty research and student learning. This would be bad enough if it were a phase or fashion, but the increasing use of biased hiring processes to weed out non-believers is creating a permanent, self-replicating staff.

To take one example, to recruit an "African American Studies professor versed in 'feminist and queer studies,'" Yale asked applicants to "share 'some way(s) in which they have championed diversity, equity, inclusion, and belonging." The requirement for evidence of "championing" DEI would screen out anyone who dares question its premise.

Similar DEI litmus tests have now infected promotions in the public sector.

Sen. Tommy Tuberville (R-AL) has drawn attention to the military's promotion into senior grades of officers who spout the required dogma about DEI, fealty to which is becoming a necessary tick-box for advancement. This is despite the fact that it does nothing to promote military readiness.

One aspiring general officer on the pending promotion list is Air Force Colonel Benjamin Jonsson, who wrote an article excoriating his fellow (white) colonels, recommending that they read "White Fragility" by Robin DiAngelo. DiAngelo's depressing thesis is that all white people are inherently racists, especially the ones who don't think they are.

Politicized Ideologues

"Replacing the officer class of police and military ranks with politicized ideologues who will bend to a transformative dogma is a strategy that has worked in places like the Soviet Union, Cuba, and Venezuela," according to the Heritage Foundation's Mike Gonzalez.

Over at the State Department, joining the ranks of the senior civil or foreign service is the civilian equivalent of becoming a general or admiral. Skill and experience are important, but reciting the right catechism plays an increasing role. The easiest path is to tell the boss what he/she/ze wants to hear, and under Joe Biden, that's DEI. Anyone questioning the existence of "systemic racism" at the State, or challenging assumptions about racial outcomes in hiring, promotion, crime, incarceration, or education, would be sidelined at some stage, no matter how solid their data or convincing their argument.

By sharing the same ideology, or at least pretending to, the elite ranks thus replicate themselves over time.

Mentoring DEI[A]

The Department of State's new "DEIA Champions Sponsorship Program" is an example of this closed loop. The program matches "mid-level mentees with senior-level sponsors/mentors" to "form a cohort of change agents who have a strong commitment to and demonstrated track record of advancing DEIA." (State adds an "A" for "accessibility.")

The main payoff for the 30 officers being mentored is that "sponsors will help them ... strengthen their competitiveness to cross the Senior Foreign Service threshold," and to be more competitive for Deputy Chief of Mission and Principle Officer jobs, the most coveted overseas assignments apart from ambassador.

Mentors, meanwhile, "will be able to point to a concrete way that they are advancing the Department's DEIA goals (a criterion for obtaining senior leadership positions)." Advancing DEI[A] is now an obligatory area in the promotion precepts for foreign service officers. It was added, thanks mostly to the State's recently departed Chief Diversity Officer, Gina Abercrombie-Winstanley.

The DEIA Champions program has sessions in Washington over the coming year, for which the State Department will pay travel costs. While the program is open to "employees of all backgrounds," selection criteria … will be based on applicants' demonstrated track record of advancing DEIA." Therefore, this taxpayer-funded program is really open only to those already committed to this contentious ideology.

Implausibly, DEIA Champions intends to "create brave spaces for candid and courageous conversations between Department leaders and program participants to discuss and develop solutions for the Department's DEIA challenges." Yet, as applicants can only be selected after showing a "demonstrated track record of advancing DEIA," the only "brave space" created will be a groupthink bubble. Any diversity of viewpoint as to the validity of DEI as a guiding principle would be ruled out from the very start.

Organizations get the behavior they reward. The military and federal government are increasingly rewarding adherence, and requiring declarations of fealty, to the divisive, discriminatory ideology of DEI. With each generation of self-replicating leadership, it will get worse. Congress needs to root out and defund DEI bureaucracies, starting with the State Department's appropriations bill, before it's too late.

DEI Training: Harmful, Phony, And Expensive

Over the years, social scientists who have conducted careful reviews of the evidence base for diversity trainings have frequently come to discouraging conclusions.

Every company has a DEI program. They cost serious money. But there's no evidence they work, and some evidence that they make things worse as shown in the Rod Dreher "DEI Training: Harmful, Phony, And Expensive" review in the January 2023 issue of *The American Conservative*.

Though diversity trainings have been around in one form or another since at least the 1960s, few of them are ever subjected to rigorous evaluation, and those that are, mostly appear to have little or no positive long-term effects.

The lack of evidence is "disappointing," wrote Elizabeth Levy Paluck of Princeton and her co-authors in a 2021 Annual Review of Psychology article, "considering the frequency with which calls for diversity training emerge in the wake of widely publicized instances of discriminatory conduct."

Dr. Paluck's team found just two large experimental studies in the previous decade that attempted to evaluate the effects of diversity trainings and met basic quality benchmarks. Other researchers have been similarly unimpressed. "We have been speaking to employers about this research for more than a decade," wrote the sociologists Frank Dobbin and Alexandra Kalev in 2018, "with the message that diversity training is likely the most expensive, and least effective, diversity program around." (To be fair, not all of these critiques apply as sharply to voluntary diversity trainings.)

If diversity trainings have no impact whatsoever, that would mean that perhaps billions of dollars are being wasted annually in the United States on these efforts.

But there's a darker possibility: Some diversity initiatives might actually worsen the D.E.I. climates of the organizations that pay for them.

That's partly because any psychological intervention may turn out to do more harm than good. The late psychologist Scott Lilienfeld made this point in an influential 2007 article where he argued that certain interventions—including ones geared at fighting youth substance use, youth delinquency and PTSD—likely fell into that category. In the case of D.E.I., Dr. Dobbin and Dr. Kalev warn that diversity trainings that are mandatory, or that threaten dominant groups' sense of belonging or make them feel blamed, may elicit negative backlash or exacerbate pre-existing biases.

Many popular contemporary D.E.I. approaches meet these criteria. They often seem geared more toward sparking a revolutionary re-understanding of race relations than solving organizations' specific problems. And they often blame white people—or their culture—for harming people of color. For example, the activist Tema Okun's work cites concepts like "objectivity" and "worship of the written word" as characteristics of "white supremacy culture."

Robin DiAngelo's "white fragility" trainings are intentionally designed to make white participants uncomfortable.

And microaggression trainings are based on an area of academic literature that claims, without quality evidence, that common utterances like "America is a melting pot" harm the mental health of people of color. Many of these trainings run counter to the views of most Americans—of any color—on race and equality. And they're generating exactly the sort of backlash that research predicts.

Of course they do. Anybody with a lick of sense knows that these things are about two things: 1) assuaging the consciences of white liberals in power, and 2) laying down markers for how power works within the organization, to justify disempowering whites on the basis of their skin color, and calling it virtue. Besides, 3) these things are never about true diversity, true equity, and true inclusion; people who don't fit the bourgeois progressive's idea of a demographic in need of special treatment don't count.

After I went through one DEI program at my then-newspaper, the white woman who oversaw the program asked me what I thought of it. I pointed out that it valorizes sham diversity. For example (I told her), there are more than a few religious conservatives in our readership area, but the only religious conservatives in this newsroom are the black Pentecostal secretaries, and me.

Nobody in authority here cares about whether or not there's a diversity of ideas in this newsroom. Whether you're white, black, Latino, or Asian, straight or gay, male or female, everybody pretty much went to the same colleges, and everybody pretty much thinks the same (liberal) way. It was phony, the whole thing. And I'm sure that white liberal diversity tsaritsa went away thinking that my objections were what you'd naturally expect from a white male whose power was threatened, and therefore my views were dismissable.

As Jesse Singal (who is a woke-skeptical progressive) notes, there is little to no evidence to support some of the nakedly ideological claims made by the DEI training leading lights. Diversity, Equity, and Inclusion cannot fail; it can only be failed. When it doesn't work, the only solution, then, is more DEI, more training, and more consultant$. And only a fool would dare to question any of this in the workplace, given how the stain of being thought of as a racist would harm one in the workplace.

When I've sat through DEI training within newsrooms, we conservatives -- not all of us white! -- would trade glances, roll our eyes, and meet afterward to complain about the bullsh*t we had just been forced to sit through. But the one thing we would never do is object to any of it, publicly. We all knew that this stuff had the force of law within corporate culture, and that to question any of it, even in good faith, was to set oneself apart as a troublemaker, and probably a racist or some other sort of bigot.

Rather than make relations between racial groups more congenial, they made non-progressive whites more suspicious and afraid of minority co-workers.

Why? Because the sessions, which felt like receiving training in dogmatic theology in a rigid, punitive seminary, made it clear who had power and who did not. One tended to avoid any potentially controversial conversation with a minority co-worker, to avoid that chance of being accused of racism, of microaggressions, or of any other offense against the sacred code. Within organizations dominated by DEI ideology, you had no reason to believe that if accused by someone favored by DEI categories, you would get a fair hearing.

The entire DEI ethos functions to make whites and people of all races who dissent into thought criminals. In one company I worked for that was all-in for DEI, it was infuriating to see minorities who were clearly not as good at their jobs as whites with more experience receive promotions, and the managers (usually white people) advancing these employees not on the basis of merit, but race, sex, or other DEI-privileged characteristic, patting themselves on the back for their virtue. In the professional circles I moved in, DEI training and the DEI mindset caused nothing but fear, suspicion, and deep cynicism about company leadership.

I suppose I should say that as far as I knew, none of my DEI-hating colleagues were against the idea of having a diverse workforce. What we objected to, in part, was that DEI was an ideology that could be used to stymie our professional advancement, no matter how hard we worked and what we achieved, because we did not have the right skin color of other demographic characteristic favored by the ideology.

And we resented that DEI was an ideology used to manage employees by inculcating fear of having your career ruined by the mere accusation of bigotry, however flimsy the evidence.

We all knew how the Human Resources department worked, and how terrified the white people running the organization were of being thought of as soft on bigotry.

You can imagine what this climate of fear does to the working of a newsroom, where doing your job well requires questioning authority, testing your hypotheses, and even risking arguments with colleagues in an effort to get to the truth.

I haven't been part of newspaper circles for some time now, but when I was, I knew conservatives and other anti-woke people throughout the industry who could read the handwriting on the wall, and who were looking for a graceful exit from newspapers before someone, somewhere, within their office accused them of sinning against DEI, and torpedoing their professional reputations.

Mind you, we didn't have the terms "woke" and "DEI" in those days, but we had the same mindset. Only now, after the *Great Awokening*, I understand that things are so much more intense, particularly with the entry into the media workforce of woke Jacobins who know how to use ideology to target older people and those they consider to be obstacles. If I were working for a newspaper now, I would be extremely cautious about challenging what woke colleagues had to say about anything, however silly or wrong-headed their position, out of fear of what they could do to me.

Singal writes:

So what does work? Robert Livingston, a lecturer at the Harvard Kennedy School who works as both a bias researcher and a diversity consultant, has a simple proposal: "Focus on actions and behaviors rather than hearts and minds."

Precisely! Does your organization have a problem with racism or other form of bigotry -- something that can be documented? Focus on fighting that. Me, I don't care if the people I work with secretly hate white people, or Christians, or conservatives.

As long as they treat me fairly, and with professional courtesy and respect, that's all I can expect. It's not the place of one's employer to police one's inner thoughts. For a company to take it upon itself to adjust the hearts and minds of its employees is something that can only create more problems than it solves.

A New Civil Rights Agenda

This year's Martin Luther King, Jr. Day was marked by contentious debate about the state of civil rights law in America. Leading the way, Christopher F. Rufo's January 2024 "A New Civil Rights Agenda" article in the *City Journal* explains why:

On the left, as always, the failure to achieve equal outcomes along racial lines requires greater state intervention. On the right, a different critique has gained traction, most notably in Christopher Caldwell's *Age of Entitlement* and Richard Hanania's *The Origins of Woke*, books arguing that American civil rights law has metastasized into a "second Constitution" that has led inexorably to left-wing racialism as the nation's new orthodoxy.

This critique has merit. The modern civil rights regime has assumed unprecedented power to reshape public and private life, regulating not only instances of outright discrimination but also the minutiae of thought, behavior, speech, and association.

The Civil Rights Act of 1964 appealed to the noble principle of equality, but over time the legal structure that it helped establish has metamorphized into an intrusive "diversity and inclusion" bureaucracy that discriminates against supposed "oppressor" groups—namely whites and Asians—and imposes left-wing ideology.

The question is what to do about it. Libertarians have long argued that the Civil Rights Act compromises core freedoms of speech and association to such a degree that only repealing the law can restore them. Another faction argues that the solution to minoritarian identity politics is majoritarian identity politics—that is, if the legal regime has become a racial spoils system, then Americans of European descent must develop "white racial consciousness" and fight for their share.

Both these approaches are misguided. Some conservatives seem to have forgotten that the Civil Rights Act was a response to state-sanctioned racial injustice in the United States and that, at its best, the civil rights movement appealed to the ideals of the Declaration of Independence and the language of the Fourteenth Amendment.

The libertarian proposal for abolishing the Civil Rights Act, like most libertarian proposals, is unfeasible. The white identity proposal, which I have previously criticized, is a recipe for permanent racial division, more akin to "prison gang politics" than republican virtue.

Happily, another avenue is open to us: reform.

The ideological capture of the Civil Rights Act is neither fixed nor inevitable. Rather than argue for its abolition, Americans concerned about the excesses of the DEI bureaucracy should appeal to higher principles and demand that our civil rights law conform to the standard of colorblind equality.

The answer to left-wing racialism is not right-wing racialism—it is the equal treatment of individuals under law, according to their talents and virtues, rather than their ancestry and anatomy. This policy does not require radical innovations. Embracing the philosophy of the American Founding—with its emphasis on natural rights and liberties—will suffice.

The only hope for a diverse nation is a regime of colorblind equality.

What would this new civil rights agenda look like in practice? First, reformers should outlaw affirmative action and racial preferences of any kind. Both policies are euphemisms for racial discrimination.

The next president should rescind Lyndon Johnson's 1965 Executive Order 11246, which established "affirmative action" and marked the initial deviation from the standard of colorblind equality. Congress should strengthen this principle by amending the language of the Civil Rights Act to make indisputably clear that the law will not permit state-sanctioned discrimination toward any racial group, whether in the minority or the majority.

Second, reformers must eliminate the "disparate impact" provisions in the Civil Rights Act of 1991 and overturn *Griggs v. Duke Power Co.*, both of which have entrenched the doctrine that disparate group outcomes are de facto evidence of racial discrimination.

This is a preposterous standard: a system of equal rights necessarily means unequal outcomes, as different groups have different preferences, talents, and capacities. Under a just system, the criterion for assessing biased treatment would not be disparate outcomes but specific, concrete discrimination, driven by animus.

Much as libel law requires actual malice, anti-discrimination law should require proof that an individual or institution sought to discriminate. The change in standard would have an immediate effect, reducing the number of frivolous lawsuits and changing the incentives that have driven institutions toward racialist ideology as a defensive strategy.

Third, legislators should abolish the DEI bureaucracies in all American institutions, which openly discriminate against disfavored racial groups, impose ideological orthodoxies on American citizens, and restrict freedoms of speech and association. In addition, federal legislators should radically reduce the size of the federal departments of civil rights enforcement.

Bureaucracies are designed to discover—or, if the supply is low, fabricate—whatever transgression they are tasked with eliminating. While a large civil rights enforcement apparatus may have been necessary to enforce non-discrimination law in the past, it is no longer necessary. Americans are a tolerant, cooperative people; a "night watchman" civil rights state and a competent courts system would be sufficient to resolve disputes and ensure compliance with the law.

3 – The Social Justice Fallacies and False Narratives of "Equity"

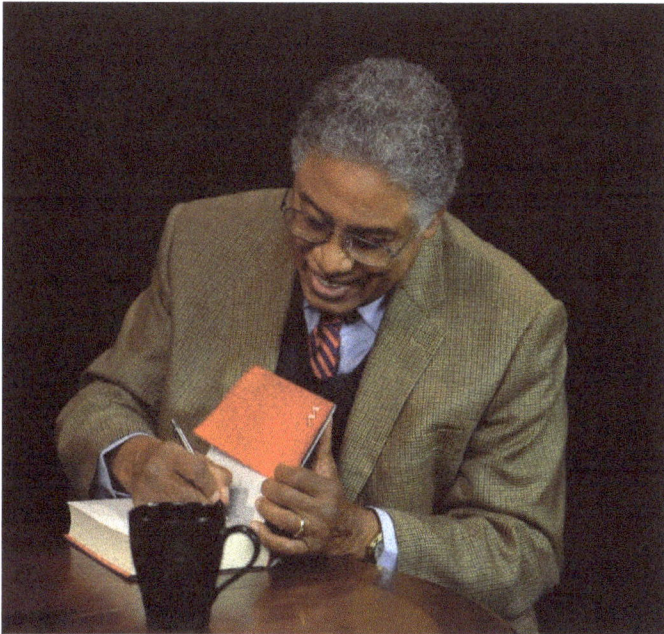

Credit: Thomas Sowell, author of Social Justice Fallacies.
Image courtesy of Basic Books.

Over the past decade, the discourse of "social justice" has ripped through the Western world, inspiring a cultural insurgency that has undermined the legitimacy of Western history, traditions, and institutions. As explored in the Edward Weech "Sowell's Summary Argument" May 2024 book review from The Russell Kirk Center of Thomas Sowell's 2023 *Social Justice Fallacies*:

Embraced by an elite caste of politicians, media figures, and government bureaucrats, the social justice ideology has made a seemingly inexorable march through public life, and become de rigueur for highly-educated

Western youth. Yet it has also provoked mounting popular disquiet, resulting in growing demand for books analyzing the "woke" phenomenon or suggesting how to arrest or simply slow the process of social and cultural change.

One of the most respected and influential figures on the American right over the past half-century, Sowell's numerous books on economics, politics, and history have made a significant contribution to conservative and libertarian thought. And here's why:

Back in the eighteenth century, Jean-Jacques Rousseau expressed the essence of the social justice vision when he wrote of "the equality which nature established among men and the inequality which they have instituted among themselves." In the kind of world envisioned by Rousseau, all classes, races and other subdivisions of the human species would have equal chances in all endeavors- other things being equal. But the more other things there are, influencing outcomes, the lower the chances of all those other things being equal.

"Equal Chances" Fallacies

In the real world, there is seldom anything resembling the equal outcomes that might be expected if all factors affecting outcomes were the same for everyone. Even in a society with equal opportunity- in the sense of judging each individual by the same standards- people from different backgrounds do not necessarily even want to do the same things, much less invest their time and energies into developing the same kinds of skills and talents.

In American sports, for example, blacks are very over-represented in professional basketball, whites in professional tennis, and Hispanics in Major League Baseball. In professional hockey, where there are more teams in the United States than in Canada, there are more Canadian players than American players- even though the population of the United States is more than eight times the population of Canada. There are also more hockey players from Sweden- nearly 4,000 miles away- in the NHL than there are hockey players from California, even though the population of California is nearly four times the population of Sweden.

Different climates are among the many other things that are not equal. Colder climates, with waterways frozen for months at a time, offer more opportunities for more people to grow up developing the ice-skating skills essential for hockey. Such climates are far more common in Canada and Sweden than in the United States in general or California in particular.

Climate Differences

Climate differences are among numerous other differences that can facilitate the development of some capabilities in particular peoples and impede the development of other capabilities.

At the heart of the social justice vision is the assumption that, because economic and other disparities among human beings greatly exceed any differences in their innate capacities, these disparities are evidence or proof of the effects of such human vices as exploitation and discrimination.

These vices are in fact among the many influences that prevent different groups of people- whether classes, races or nations- from having equal, or even comparable, outcomes in economic terms or other terms. But human vices have no monopoly as causes of economic and other disparities.

It is especially difficult to make the case that inequalities of outcomes can be automatically assumed to have been caused by discrimination by dominant majorities against subordinate minorities, when in fact many subordinate minorities have economically outperformed dominant majorities in many countries around the world and in many periods of history.

By contrast, we can read reams of social justice literature without encountering a single example of the proportional representation of different groups in endeavors open to competition- in any country in the world today, or at any time over thousands of years of recorded history.

Among the many factors that can prevent equal human potentialities from producing equally developed capabilities are factors over which humans have very little control-such as geography-and other factors over which humans have no control at all, such as the past. There are innumerable things that can create unequal chances, some of which are worth examining in some detail.

Reciprocal Inequalities

While group equalities in the same endeavors are by no means common, adds Sowell, what is common are reciprocal inequalities among groups in different endeavors. The equality among different groups of human beings-presupposed by those who regard disparities in outcomes as evidence or proof of discriminatory bias-might well be true as regards innate potentialities.

But people are not hired or paid for their innate potentialities. They are hired, paid, admitted to colleges or accepted into other desired positions on the basis of their developed capabilities relevant to the particular endeavor. In these terms, reciprocal inequalities might suggest equal potentialities, without providing any basis for expecting equal outcomes.

Even groups lagging in many kinds of achievement tend nevertheless to have some particular endeavors where they do not merely hold their own but excel. Groups lacking in their educational backgrounds, for example, may lag in many other endeavors, for which such a background is essential-and yet such generally lagging groups have often excelled in some other endeavors, where personal talent and dedication are key factors. Sports and entertainment have long been among such endeavors with high achievements for such American groups rising out of poverty as the Irish, blacks and Southern whites.

While group equality- in either incomes or capabilities-is hard to find, it is also hard to find any ethnic or other large social group that has no endeavor in which it is above average.

Reciprocal Inequalities in Action

Reciprocal inequalities abound- even when equality does not. As we have seen, different ethnic groups dominate different American sports. One consequence of this is that the degree of inequality of group representation in American sports as a whole is not as severe as in each individual sport. A similar principle applies, for similar reasons, in other endeavors, because of reciprocal inequalities.

If one looks at wealthy, historic individuals in commerce and industry, for example, one could find Jews far more widely represented among historic leaders in retailing, finance and garment production and sales than in the steel industry, automobile production or coal mining. In the professions as well, groups that have similar representation in the professions as a whole can have very different representations in particular professions, such as engineering, medicine or the law. Asian American professionals are not necessarily concentrated in the same professions as Irish American professionals.

Because of reciprocal inequalities, the more narrowly defined the endeavor, the less likely are different groups to be comparably represented.

Yet crusaders for social justice often decry uneven representation of groups in an individual company, as evidence or proof of employer discrimination in that particular company.

When different peoples evolve differently in very different settings and conditions, they can develop different talents that create reciprocal inequalities of achievements in a wide range of endeavors, without necessarily creating equality, or even comparability, in any of those endeavors. Such reciprocal inequalities lend no support to theories of either genetic determinism or discriminatory biases as automatic explanations of inequalities.

Women Are Statistically "Under-Represented "in Silicon Valley

Many assumptions and phrases in the social justice literature are repeated endlessly, without any empirical test. When women are statistically "under-represented "in Silicon Valley, for example, some people automatically assume that to be due to sex discrimination by Silicon Valley employers. It so happens that the work done in Silicon Valley is based on an application of engineering skills, including computer software engineering- and American women receive less than 30 percent of the degrees in engineering, whether at the college level or the postgraduate level.

When American men receive less than 20 percent of the undergraduate degrees in education, and only 22 percent and 32 percent of master's degrees and doctoral degrees, respectively, in the same subject, is it surprising that men are under-represented among school teachers and women are under-represented in engineering occupations?

Comparing the statistical representation of women and men in either of these occupations is like comparing apples and oranges, when their educational specializations are so different. These educational specialization decisions were usually made individually, years before either the women or the men reached an employer to begin a professional career.

A more general question arises when the incomes of women as a whole are compared to the incomes of men as a whole. This leaves out many specific differences in the life patterns of women and men. One of the most basic of these differences is that women are full-time, year-round workers significantly less often than men.

15 Million More Male, Full-time, Year-Round Workers

U.S. Census Bureau data show that, in 2019, there were 15 million more male, full-time, year-round workers than female, full-time, year-round workers. The work patterns of women include more part-time work, and some whole years when many women are out of the labor force entirely, often due to staying home to take care of young children.

When these and other differences in work patterns are taken into account, male-female differences in income shrink drastically, and in some cases reverse. As far back as 1971, single women in their thirties who had worked continuously since leaving school were earning slightly more than men of the same description.

When there are statistical differences in the representation of various ethnic groups, different patterns within these groups themselves are likewise often overlooked. A typical example of equating differences in demographic representation with employer discrimination was a headline in a San Francisco newspaper: Why are Black and Latino people still kept out of tech industry?

Are Asians "Kept Out" of Professional Basketball?

Are Asians "kept out" of professional basketball or Californians "kept out" of the National Hockey League? Is equal demographic representation so widespread or so automatic in other endeavors that its absence in a particular endeavor can only be due to someone keeping particular people out?

As in the case of sex differences in demographic representation in an engineering endeavor, ethnic differences in educational qualifications for an engineering career are blatant. Asian Americans have more college degrees in engineering than either blacks or Hispanics, each of whom outnumbers Asian Americans in the U.S. population. At the Ph.D. level, Asian Americans' engineering degrees outnumber the engineering Ph.D.'s of blacks and Hispanics put together.

The "disparate impact "standard, used by courts of law for determining employer discrimination, implicitly assumes something that no one can seem to find anywhere- equal demographic representation of different groups. Any number of scholarly international studies have found gross disparities common in countries around the world. One of these studies concluded: "In no society have all regions and all parts of the population developed equally."

Nevertheless, some Justices of the U.S. Supreme Court have accepted "disparate impact" statistics as evidence or proof of employer discrimination, even though the Supreme Court itself has had statistical disparities more extreme than the disparities used to charge employers with discrimination. For eight consecutive years- from 2010 to 2017-all Supreme Court Justices were either Catholic or Jewish, in a country where Protestants outnumber Catholics and Jews combined. Yet one of the most obvious reasons for doubting any negative intention or conspiracy is that these Justices were appointed by Presidents of both political parties, and all those Presidents were Protestants.

None of this denies that employer biases are a factor that can be, and has been, responsible for some disparities in employment outcomes. But human biases have no monopoly among the many things that prevent "equal chances."

Origins of Inequalities

The question whether different social groups have equal or unequal capabilities in various endeavors is very different from the question whether racial or sexual differences create inherently different mental potential determined by genes adds Sowell. The genetic determinism assumption that reigned supreme among American intellectuals of the Progressive era in the early twentieth century is an irrelevant issue in this context and has been dealt with more extensively elsewhere.

If we assume, for the sake of argument, that every social group- or even every individual- has equal mental potential at the moment of conception, that would still not be enough to guarantee even equal "native intelligence" at birth, much less equally developed capabilities after growing up in unequal circumstances and/or being culturally oriented toward different goals in different fields.

Inequalities Among Individuals

Unequal circumstances begin in the womb. Research has shown nutritional differences among pregnant women reflected later in IQ differences among their children, when these children were old enough to be tested. Mothers' intakes of various substances can have positive or negative effects on a child's IQ and general well- being.

Even where we might reasonably expect to find the greatest equality of developed capabilities- among children born to the same parents and raised in the same home- research going back as far as the nineteenth century, and including countries on both sides of the Atlantic, has shown that children who are the first-born in their family have, as a group, higher average IQs, a higher rate of college completion, and are over-represented among high achievers in a variety of endeavors.

In the United States, for example, a study found that more than half the National Merit Scholarship finalists were a first-born child, even in five-child families, as well as in two-child, three-child and four-child families. In other words, in five-child families, the first-born was the finalist more often than the other four siblings combined.

First-Born and Only Child

Other measures of educational success or career success have likewise shown the first-born-and an only child- to be over-represented among the top performers in various endeavors, whether in the United States or among top performers in other countries surveyed.

The first-born, or an only child, can have the undivided attention of both parents during a child's crucial earliest development. This is something which later siblings obviously cannot have.

Conversely, children raised where there is only one parent present have been found in a number of studies to have a higher incidence of many social problems- again, both in the United States and on the other side of the Atlantic, studies of boys raised without a father present have found them very much over-represented among people with pathologies ranging from truancy to murder.

As one study put it, these pathologies were more highly correlated with fatherlessness than with any other factor, "surpassing even race and poverty." Fatherless boys had a higher than average rate of incarceration, whether they were black or white, though the incidence of fatherless boys has been higher among blacks. Not all differences between races are due to race either in the sense of genetics or in the sense of racial discrimination.

Clearly, there were no "equal chances" for these boys, whether they were treated fairly or unfairly by people they encountered in institutions ranging from schools to police departments. Girls were also affected negatively, as reflected in such things as higher rates of teenage pregnancy, when raised by one parent.

Very similar patterns of pathology were found in England, where the ethnic makeup of the underclass population is very different from that in the United States. In England, the underclass is predominantly white, but it shows many social patterns very similar to the social patterns of low-income blacks in the United States, even though the English underclass has no "legacy of slavery" to be used as an automatic explanation.

Children Raised in Families on Welfare

When American children are raised in different social classes, with different child-rearing practices, the chances of these children growing up with equal capabilities in adulthood can be seriously reduced. Research has shown that children raised by parents with professional occupations hear more than three times as many words per hour as children raised in families on welfare. Moreover, these are far more often positive and encouraging words when the parents are professionals, and more often negative and discouraging words when the family is on welfare.

Can anyone seriously believe that children spending their formative years growing up in homes this different are likely to be the same as others in school, on a job or elsewhere?

In putting assumptions to the test of facts, a clear distinction must be maintained between equal potentialities at the beginning of life and equally developed capabilities later on. Some social justice advocates may implicitly assume that various groups have similar developed capabilities, so that different outcomes appear puzzling.

But, when it comes to actual performance capabilities, a man is not even equal to himself- either physically or mentally- at different stages of his life, much less equal to all other people in their varying stages of life.

Inequalities Among Groups

The seemingly invincible fallacy at the heart of the social justice vision is that large categories of people- classes, races, nations- would tend to be either equal, or at least comparable, in their outcomes in various endeavors, if it were not for some discriminatory bias that has intervened to produce the large disparities we see around us.

Yet different groups, with different median ages-vary by a decade or two- are unlikely to be equal in endeavors requiring either the physical vitality of youth or the experience that comes with age. When Japanese Americans have a median age of 52 and Mexican Americans have a median age of 28, their different representation in different occupations and at different income levels is hardly surprising.

If these two groups were identical in every other respect, age differences alone would still be enough to make them differ in incomes, since middle-aged Americans have higher median incomes than Americans in their twenties.

With nations-as with classes, races or ethnic groups-age differences alone are enough to make equal economic or other outcomes very unlikely.

There are whole nations whose populations have a median age over 40 (Germany, Italy, Japan), and other nations whose median ages are under 20 (Nigeria, Afghanistan, Angola).

Why should anyone expect a nation where half the population are infants, young children and teenagers to have the same work experience and education-the same human capital-as a nation where half the population is 40 years old or older?

Different nations are also located in different geographic, climatic and other settings, with different advantages and disadvantages. Even if their populations had identical potential, they could hardly be expected to have equally developed capabilities, after centuries of being confronted with the task of surviving and evolving in very different settings around the world.

Whole continents differ greatly from one another. Although Africa is more than twice the size of Europe, the European coastline is thousands of kilometers longer than the African coastline. This might seem to be almost impossible. But the European coastline has innumerable twists and turns, creating harbors where ships can dock safely, sheltered from the rough waters of the open seas. These harbors are an even bigger advantage than the longer coastline as such.

The European Coastline

The European coastline is also increased by the many islands and peninsulas that make up more than one- third of that continent's total land area. By contrast, the African coastline is smooth, with far fewer harbors and far fewer islands and peninsulas- which make up only 2 percent of Africa's land area.

Is it surprising that Europeans have long had the benefit of far more maritime trade than Africans? Adam Smith noted this geographic difference back in the eighteenth century, and he also rejected claims that Africans were racially inferior. Other scholars have likewise described the numerous and severe geographic handicaps of sub-Saharan Africa especially. Distinguished French historian Fernand Braudel concluded: "In understanding Black Africa, geography is more important than history."

Harbors are just one of the various kinds of navigable waterways with major implications for the economic and social development of human beings. That is because of the enormous difference in costs between water transportation and land transportation. In the ancient world, for example, the cost of transporting a cargo across the length of the Mediterranean Sea- more than 2,000 miles- was less than the cost of transporting that same cargo just 75 miles inland. This meant that people living on the coast had a vastly larger range of economic and social interactions with other coastal people and places than people living inland had with other people living inland or with their coastal compatriots.

A geographic treatise noted that, in ancient times, Europe's Mediterranean hinterland was "lingering in a backward civilization as compared with the Mediterranean coastland."

Nor was this peculiar to the Mediterranean region. It has been common in various parts of the world that "the coasts of a country are the first parts to develop, not an indigenous or local civilization, but a cosmopolitan culture, which later spreads inland from the seaboard." There have been special exceptions, but this has been a general pattern.

This pattern reflected the great difference between the cost of water transportation and land transportation, which in turn affects economic prospects in many ways. Most of the large cities around the world are located on navigable waterways, because transporting the huge volume of food required to keep people fed in those cities would be enormously more expensive if all food had to be transported solely over land- especially before the modern invention of railroads and trucks during the past two centuries.

Even today, places with access to navigable rivers have great economic advantages, especially if these are navigable rivers that connect to coastal areas.

Climate

Climate is another aspect of nature that can influence the economic and social development of human beings. Fertile soils are found more often in the temperate zones than in the tropics. This obviously affects the productivity of agriculture. But its effects do not end there. Urbanization depends on food supplied from outside urban communities, with agriculture usually being the primary source. Over the centuries, a wholly disproportionate share of advances in science, technology and other endeavors have originated in urban communities.

An empirical study at Harvard's Center for International Development found that places in the temperate zone, with fertile soil and located within 100 kilometers of the sea, were 8 percent of the world's inhabited land area. But such places had 23 percent of the world's population and produced 53 percent of the world's Gross Domestic Product. This is reflected in worldwide differences in income per person between such places and the rest of the world.

This is just one of many differences among the world's geographic regions. When Europeans arrived in the Western Hemisphere, the indigenous peoples had no horses, oxen, camels or elephants, nor any other heavy-duty draft animals or beasts of burden to provide transportation for people and cargoes, such as animals provided in much of the Eastern Hemisphere. Llamas existed in the Inca empire in part of South America, where they were used as beasts of burden. But even in that fraction of South America where llamas existed, they were not large enough to be comparable to the animals used in the other half of the world.

Draft Animals and Beasts of Burden

The dearth of draft animals and beasts of burden in the Western Hemisphere had wider economic implications. By making land transportation even more costly than usual, the lack of animals limited the distances where it was economically feasible to transport cargoes. This in turn also limited the size of vessels for water transportation. Canoes were common in the Western Hemisphere. But vessels of the size of European ships, or the even larger ships in China during Europe's Middle Ages, were not economically viable without animals to transport the vast cargoes, from miles around, required to fill such ships.

Nor were wheeled vehicles used in the Western Hemisphere before Europeans arrived. The wheel has sometimes been considered an epoch-making invention for economic development. But wheeled vehicles, without animals to pull them, had no such potential. The Mayans invented wheels, but they were used on children's toys. Had the Mayans been in communication with the Incas and their llamas, conceivably wheeled vehicles, pulled by animals, might have become an economic asset in the

Western Hemisphere. But geographic limitations on the size of a cultural universe in the Western Hemisphere at that time prevented the creation of such a development.

When the British confronted the Iroquois in North America, these were peoples drawing upon very different-sized cultural universes. Although the Iroquois were a confederation of tribes living in a large area, the animals present on the vast Eurasian landmass- and absent in the Western Hemisphere- gave the British access to the inventions, discoveries and knowledge from far wider regions of the world.

The British were able to navigate across the ocean by using the compass, invented in China, steering with rudders invented in China, doing calculations with mathematical concepts from Egypt, using a numbering system invented in India, and writing on paper invented in China, using letters created by the Romans.

The Iroquois had no comparable access to the cultural achievements of the Incas or the Mayans. Nor did they have as wide an exposure to the many diseases that spread across the vast Eurasian landmass- spanning more than 10,000 kilometers- creating devastating epidemics in centuries past, but leaving the surviving populations in Europe with biological resistance to many diseases, whose germs they took with them to the Western Hemisphere.

There those diseases devastated many indigenous populations, who lacked biological resistance to those diseases. Death rates, sometimes exceeding 50 percent or more, among the indigenous peoples facilitated the European conquest of North and South America.

Neither with geographic factors nor other aspects of nature can we automatically assume either equal or random outcomes among human beings. There are too many factors at work to expect them all to be equal, or to have remained equal over the thousands of years in which human beings have developed economically and socially.

Nature

Nature- as exemplified by such things as differences in geography, climate, diseases and animals- has not been egalitarian, despite Rousseau's claim that nature produced equality. As distinguished economic historian David

S. Landes put it, "nature like life is unfair" and "The world has never been a level playing field."

Western Europe and Northern Europe have long had more of the natural resources used in an industrial revolution- iron ore and coal, for example- than did Eastern Europe or Southern Europe. But none of that mattered during the many thousands of years before human beings' knowledge developed to the point where they were capable of creating an industrial revolution. Which part of Europe was more advantaged or disadvantaged varied with particular eras, and the human knowledge available in those eras.

Nature has been no more fair between the sexes than in its treatment of other social groups, societies or nations. Human double standards of sexual behavior for women and men have been a pale reflection of nature's more fundamental double standards. No matter how reckless, selfish, stupid or irresponsible a man may be, he will never become pregnant. The plain and simple fact that women have babies has meant that they may not have equal chances in many other aspects of life, even when some human societies offer equal opportunity for people with the same developed capabilities.

The seemingly invincible fallacy that only human bias can explain different economic and social outcomes among peoples is belied repeatedly by hard facts in societies around the world. Whatever the condition of human beings at the beginning of the species, scores of millennia had already come and gone before anyone coined the phrase "social justice."

During those almost unimaginably vast expanses of time, different peoples evolved differently in very different settings around the world- developing different talents that created reciprocal inequalities of achievements in different endeavors, without necessarily creating equality, or even comparability, in any of those endeavors.

Conclusion

Do we want the mixture of students who are going to be trained to do advanced medical research to be representative of the demographic make-up of the population as a whole- or do we want whatever students, from whatever background, who have track records demonstrating a mastery of medical science that gives them the highest probability of finding cures for cancer, Alzheimer's and other devastating diseases?

Endeavors have purposes. Is indulging ideological visions more important than ending cancer and Alzheimer's?

Do you want airlines to have pilots chosen for demographic representation of various groups, or would you prefer to fly on planes whose pilots were chosen for their mastery of all the complex things that increase your chances of arriving safely at your destination? Once we recognize the many factors that can create different developed capabilities, "equal chances for all" becomes very different in its consequences from "equal opportunity."

And consequences matter-or should matter-more so than some attractive or fashionable theory. More fundamentally, do we want a society in which some babies are born into the world as heirs of pre- packaged grievances against other babies born the same day-blighting both their lives-or do we want to at least leave them the option to work things out better in their lives than we have in ours?

4 – The Racist Aspect of the "Equity" Portion of DEI Policies

Credit: Interaction Institute for Social Change, Artist: Angus Maguire
@interactioninstitute.org.

The message of the cartoon above is clear: Rigidly identical standards may perpetuate inequity if we don't account for differences across personal circumstances. Seems like a rational position, policy, and point-of-view until you look more closely at who and what the boxes on the "Equity" side represent.

Diversity, equity and inclusion programs have come under attack in American boardrooms, state legislatures and college campuses—and now broadly across the federal government.

President Donald Trump hours after swearing in began making good on promises to wage a war against such policies, inking an executive order banning efforts such as "environmental justice programs," "equity initiatives" and DEI considerations in federal hiring.

According to the Nicquel Terry Ellis "What is DEI, and Why is it Dividing America?" CNN report in January 2025:

The fledgling Republican White House also ordered employees of federal diversity, equity, inclusion and accessibility offices to be put on paid administrative leave. And DEI is in the crosshairs of Trump's new Department of Government Efficiency (DOGE), led by billionaire Elon Musk, who called DEI "just another word for racism."

What is DEI, and Why is it Dividing America?

The changes come as wealthy corporate leaders, including billionaire hedge fund manager Bill Ackman and conservative activist Robby Starbuck, have decried diversity programs on social media. In step, some US companies—including the nation's largest employer, Walmart—have backpedaled on some DEI initiatives, including racial equity training programs for staff and evaluations designed to boost supplier diversity.

DEI Incompetence

DEI has also been used to criticize and discredit high-ranking lawmakers and local officials. Most recently, in the wake of the deadly Los Angeles County wildfires, Los Angeles Fire Chief Kristin Crowley came under attack for her focus on DEI efforts in the department including recruiting a more diverse force.

"DEI means people die," Musk said in an X post, resharing a local news story about Crowley being the department's first female chief.

Scott Jennings, a CNN political commentator, also condemned Crowley.

"We have DEI, we have budget cuts and yet I'm wondering now, if your house was burning down, how much do you care what color the firefighters are?" Jennings said on CNN's "News Night with Abby Phillip."

Former Vice President Kamala Harris also became a target for conservatives.

Last July, Tennessee Republican Rep. Tim Burchett suggested President Joe Biden selected Harris as his running mate because she was Black. "One hundred percent she is a DEI hire," Burchett said. "Her record is abysmal at best."

Amid the rising right-wing pressure, US workers in November viewed DEI more negatively than they did the prior year: While 52% said focusing on increasing DEI was mainly a good thing, 21% said it was a bad thing—a 5 percentage point increase from 2023—a Pew Research Center survey found.

Still, 52% of employed US adults said in 2023 they had DEI trainings or meetings at work, and 33% said they had a designated staff member who promotes DEI, a Pew survey that year found.

Critics say DEI programs are discriminatory and attempt to solve racial discrimination by disadvantaging other groups, particularly White Americans. But supporters and industry experts insist the decades-old practice has been politicized and is widely misunderstood.

What is DEI?

Among seven DEI experts and industry leaders CNN has interviewed, most had a shared vision for what constitutes the concept:

Diversity is embracing the differences everyone brings to the table, whether those are someone's race, age, ethnicity, religion, gender, sexual orientation, physical ability or other aspects of social identity.

Equity is treating everyone fairly and providing equal opportunities.

Inclusion is respecting everyone's voice and creating a culture in which people from all backgrounds feel encouraged to express their ideas and perspectives.

DEI was created because marginalized communities have not always had equal opportunities for jobs or felt a sense of belonging in majority-White corporate settings, said Daniel Oppong, founder of The Courage Collective, a consultancy that advises companies on DEI.

"That is the genesis of why some of these programs exist," he said. "It was an attempt to try to create workplaces where more or all people can thrive."

When did workplaces start embracing DEI?

The backlash against DEI may feel like a pendulum swing from 2020, when the nation faced a racial reckoning after Black father George Floyd was killed in Minneapolis by a White police officer.

But the DEI practice has been around for decades.

The origins of DEI programs date to the Civil Rights Movement, which played a pivotal role in accelerating efforts to create more diverse and inclusive workplaces, said Dominique Hollins, founder of the DEI consulting firm WĒ360.

The Civil Rights Act of 1964

The Civil Rights Act of 1964 outlawed employment discrimination based on race, religion, sex, color and national origin. It also banned segregation in public places, like public schools and libraries. And Title VII of the Civil Rights Act established the Equal Employment Opportunity Commission, or EEOC, which works to eliminate employment discrimination.

In the 1960s and '70s, employees began filing discrimination lawsuits with the EEOC, and many companies started incorporating diversity into their business strategies by providing diversity training, according to a 2008 report published in the Academy of Management Learning & Education.

These diversity training efforts emerged around the time affirmative action began by executive order from President John F. Kennedy, a Democrat. Although the concepts may seem similar, affirmative action is different from DEI as it required federal contractors by executive order to treat applicants and employees equally based on race, color, religion and sex.

Colleges and universities also used affirmative action to boost enrollment of students of color at majority-White schools. But the US Supreme Court in 2023 gutted affirmative action, ruling race-conscious college admissions were unconstitutional.

Some diversity efforts lost momentum after GOP President Ronald Reagan in the 1980s backed corporate deregulation policies asserting companies should address discrimination internally, Hollins said. In the coming decades, many companies kept pushing for DEI-focused jobs and training in a "piecemeal" fashion, rather than by creating ongoing programs and dedicated teams, she said.

Other companies didn't have the staffing or resources to sustain DEI efforts, Hollins said.

Then, Floyd's murder renewed the push for DEI leadership roles and initiatives at major corporations. Between 2019 and 2022, chief diversity and inclusion officer roles grew by 168.9%, a LinkedIn analysis found.

Now, though, some of those efforts have been rolled back and DEI roles abandoned because leaders didn't feel fully supported, Hollins said: Companies "were giving the appearance of commitment without actually doing the right work for that commitment to be sustainable."

What does DEI look like at work?

DEI in the workplace can be a mix of employee training, resource networks and recruiting practices, said Kelly Baker, executive vice president and chief human resources officer at Thrivent, an organization that provides financial advice.

In 2023, 61% of US adults said their workplace had policies focusing on fairness in hiring, promotions or pay, a Pew study that year found.

Thrivent, for example, has resource groups for women in leadership, young professionals, Black employees, Hispanic employees and military veterans, among others, Baker told CNN in a previous interview.

Its DEI trainings teach employees how to understand and bridge cultural differences in the workplace, she said, adding Thrivent also seeks job candidates with diversity in their race, geography, gender and industry background.

Many corporations tie DEI to their business strategies, experts told CNN.

Diversity "is related to our business growth strategy," Baker said. "It's pragmatic and essential and critical for us to ensure that our client base reflects the world that we are in and the world that we are going to be in."

What are critics saying?

In recent years, DEI has become a social and political lightning rod for lawmakers, corporate leaders and conservative activists who have sought to cast such initiatives as unfair and even racist, with some emboldened by the Supreme Court's gutting of affirmative action.

"These are not neutral programs to increase demographic diversity; they are political programs that use taxpayer resources to advance a specific partisan orthodoxy," outspoken DEI critic Christopher Rufo, a senior fellow at the Manhattan Institute, wrote in a 2023 *New York Times* op-ed.

Indeed, the ideology behind DEI is "fundamentally anti-American," said Ryan P. Williams, president of The Claremont Institute, a conservative think tank.

"The words that the acronym 'DEI' represent sound nice, but it is nothing more than affirmative action and racial preferences by a different name, a system that features racial headcounts and arbitrarily assigned roles of 'oppressor' and 'oppressed' groups in America," Williams said in an emailed statement. "If we continue to do democracy this way, it will only end in acrimony, strife, resentment, and American collapse."

Some critics argue DEI programs on college campuses have failed to protect Jewish students and faculty from antisemitic bullying and harassment. A 2024 Stanford University report highlighted a case in which Jewish staff reported being pressured to join the DEI program's "whiteness accountability" affinity group.

"They alleged that the program erased Jewish identity," the report said. "There was no space for these Jewish employees to share their lived experience, to raise their concerns about anti-Semitism."

Ackman, the billionaire investor, posted a 4,000-word opus on X criticizing DEI as "inherently a racist and illegal movement in its implementation even if it purports to work on behalf of the so-called oppressed." Musk, the Trump confidant and billionaire Tesla and SpaceX CEO, later reposted it on X, which he owns.

"DEI is just another word for racism. Shame on anyone who uses it," Musk wrote, later doubling down: "DEI, because it discriminates on the basis of race, gender and many other factors, is not merely immoral, it is also illegal."

Tesla since then omitted all language regarding minority workers and outreach to minority communities in a Securities and Exchange Commission filing.

Who's defending DEI practices?

Not every business leader agrees: Mark Cuban, billionaire and minority owner of the Dallas Mavericks, pushed back on Musk's posts in a thread defending DEI.

"The loss of DEI-Phobic companies is my gain," Cuban wrote. "Having a workforce that is diverse and representative of your stakeholders is good for business."

Companies turning their backs on strategies to promote diversity will limit equal opportunities for people who face disadvantages because of their skin color, the neighborhood they grew up in, the quality of schools they attended and other forces beyond their control, two Black pioneering business leaders—former Merck CEO Ken Frazier and former American Express CEO Ken Chenault—told CNN.

"At its best, DEI is about developing talent, measuring it in a fair way and finding hidden talent and disadvantaged talent in a world where not everybody has an equal chance to exhibit their abilities," Frazier said.

SHRM Eliminates "Equity" From its Focused Programming

Many in the HR member community were shocked, angry and dismayed by the announcement by SHRM they were eliminating equity from its focused programming according to the Sheila Callaham *Forbes* "Does SHRM'S Removal Of 'Equity' From Inclusion, Equity And Diversity Point To A New Strategy Or Signal Something Much Bigger?" July 2024 article below.

The Society for Human Resource Management (SHRM), the largest professional human resources membership association with nearly 340,000 members in 180 countries, made a statement earlier this month that left many of its HR member community shocked, angry and dismayed. In a statement on LinkedIn, SHRM announced that the organization was officially eliminating Equity from Inclusion, Equity and Diversity and would lead the effort with Inclusion and Diversity instead.

"Effective immediately, SHRM will be adopting the acronym "I&D" instead of "IE&D." This strategic decision underscores our commitment to leading with Inclusion as the catalyst for holistic change in workplaces and society."

The announcement came just days after the annual SHRM conference and left many members demanding to know why this major shift was not addressed at the conference and why its members–and practitioners in the field–were not asked for input.

Made on the same day as Black Women's Equal Pay Day, SHRM's timing only added to the scorn directed at the organization and its CEO, Johnny C. Taylor. SHRM's LinkedIn post about the change in strategy had almost 1,000 comments and more than 400 shares–the majority angry and raw–at the time of this publication.

"Why not poll your paying members before blurting this out for all the world to see?! Any thought on how this announcement will impact the work of those of us with boots on the ground?" wrote Dr. Tania M. Session, who works with company leaders to create psychologically safe and civil workplaces through equity, inclusion, belonging, well-being and trust.

"You're irreparably, irredeemably, broken," wrote talent acquisition leader Keirsten Greggs. In a private query for this article asking why SHRM would make such a pivotal shift without involving its members for comment, Greggs wrote, "Such an exercise would be antithetical for an organization who, instead of recognizing Black Women's Equal Pay Day, announced a shift in which equity –fairness, justice and access to advancement for all people, would be absorbed under a broader definition of inclusion."

Black women only make 64 cents for every dollar that white, non-Hispanic men make. White women make 89 cents. Included in the workplace, but far from equal. [However, numerous and credible studies consistently show the difference in wages is the natural consequence of choices that men and women freely make—not discrimination.]

Is Equity a Fundamental in Creating a Fair and Just Workplace?

"Equity is a fundamental pillar in creating a fair and just workplace," added Christopher Bylone van Sandwyk, global head of belonging, inclusion, diversity, equity and accessibility for Krispy Creme. "By removing it, SHRM sends a message that the structural inequalities and systemic barriers many individuals face are not worth addressing."

There has even been a petition for HR voices opposing SHRM, citing that SHRM has a corporate bias and favors employers at the expense of workers. Created by the Equitable HR Guild, the petition calls on HR professionals to support efforts to promote more equitable and inclusive HR practices by divesting from SHRM and reducing SHRM's influence in favor of a more equitable HR.

In other comments, members threaten to leave the organization and allow their SHRM certifications to lapse or look elsewhere for accreditation.

One lonely voice of support amongst the cries of outrage came from Kurt Miller, executive director for Northwest Public Power Association. Miller acknowledged that most comments were negative and suggested that several important considerations were being ignored.

"As someone who very much supports diversity and inclusion, I think it's critical we recognize some stark realities: One is that many people outside of HR circles view the *equity* component as one that's highly arbitrary and can lead to unfair treatment of majority groups. We cannot deny there has been a significant public backlash against the *E* which threatens to throw the baby out with the bath water."

Miller goes on to point out the Supreme Court's 2023 ruling against affirmative action in higher education and how that action has made some traditional DEI strategies are now litigious. The *Harvard Business Review* (HBR) noted the fallout from the ruling, resulting in "a barrage of challenges against workplace DEI efforts."

The article *HBR* article "DEI Is Under Attack. Here's How Companies Can Mitigate the Legal Risks" (see Chapter 9 for this article), published in January 2025, warns employers of long-standing DEI policies and procedures that could put them at risk of litigation. Those most at risk, according to the article, meet three criteria:

1. It confers a preference, meaning some individuals are treated more favorably than others.

2. The preference is given to members of a legally protected group, such as groups defined by the categories protected in Title VII of the Civil Rights Act of 1964. These are race, color, religion, national origin, and sex (including sexual orientation and gender identity).

3. The preference relates to a tangible benefit, such as a job, promotion, pay raise, work assignment, or access to training and development opportunities.

These at-risk criteria are at the core of most *equity* initiatives, meant to level the playing field for historically disenfranchised groups. HBR warns DEI programs at risk are those that still include hiring quotas, tiebreaker decision-making (i.e., when choosing between two similarly strong candidates and one is white and the other is a person of color, picking the person of color), group-specific internships and fellowships (i.e., internships excluding white people) and tying manager compensation to diversity goals.

A Failed Strategy

In an interview with Jessica Kriegel, Chief Scientist of Workplace Culture at Culture Partner, Taylor insists SHRM is executing a corrective business strategy to address the failed initiative. He recounted his talks with CEOs and referenced the extensive research SHRM has conducted since 2018, indicating that DEI has yet to produce the desired results.

Taylor is adamant that, despite increasing pressure on DEI as a practice, the goals can still be achieved—but not using the same strategies. He claims his actions are like those of any other CEO who, when faced with a failed strategy, has to decide whether to throw in the towel or regroup and try again.

"We are not going to keep doing the same thing that we've done for 30 years and expect things to be better," he told Kriegel. "We decided to focus on those things we think will help move this conversation further. After all, it's about the work, not the acronym."

Americans Are More Diverse and More Divided Than Ever

Taylor recognizes that Americans are more diverse and, sadly, more divided than ever. Progress depends on meeting people where they are and working within those parameters to create change because "everyone needs to feel included, seen, heard and valued, and that's why we lead with inclusion."

According to Gallup, "less than three in 10 employees (28%) strongly agree that their organization is fair to everyone. This is concerning, as it's hard to imagine a team being productive or effective when unfair treatment is commonplace."

That's precisely the point Taylor is trying to make.

As much as DEI may be a failed strategy, so perhaps is the way SHRM communicated this major shift in strategy. In a request for comment around how he would heal the fragmentation resulting from the announcement, Taylor responded that SHRM is committed to progress and hopes to bring the community with them.

He clarified that SHRM's announcement strategy ensured the news was shared with all members on the same channel since less than ten percent of members attended the annual conference. He also defended SHRM's research insights as always including members' feedback.

"Not surprisingly, our diverse membership has a diversity of perspectives on this topic–and most all topics in our practice."

Even within the Black community, Taylor expressed a diversity of perspectives and warned that suggesting the Black community feels one way or the other about this is a mistake.

"The generalizations many make about what the Black community supposedly wants or thinks about any topic (including DEI) is misguided; our community is not monolithic. There are several examples of organizations led by Black leaders where "Equity" is not included in their nomenclature. John Deere's SVP/CHRO is a Black Woman; the Chief People of Officer of Pinterest is a Black Woman; the CHRO of PWC is a Black Woman; and I am a Black Man—just to name a few. *None* of us have Equity or DEI in our titles or organizational or departmental titles, yet all of us are 100% committed to creating a world of work that works for all."

Taylor said members can expect an updated playbook publishing soon on SHRM's I&D page, with new articles and resources. Additionally, he said the November INCLUSION event will include a track on equity in action.

Disagreeing, With Civility

In Taylor's interview with Kriegel, she asked about the emotional impact of being the face of anti-equity—especially as a black man.

"Very honestly, what bothered me through these last ten days was not that people disagreed, but the things that they would say online about me, about SHRM, about my family—it was really personal. Why can't we just disagree? It's painful to hear, the incivility, the vitriol, the assuming that you come at this from a bad place given my personal body of work and as an African-American."

Some harsh criticism is linked to Taylor's association with Donald Trump. In February 2018, then-President Trump announced the appointment of Taylor as chairman of the president's board of advisors for historically black colleges and universities (HBCUs), adding that Taylor's appointment was "very important, and very important to me and the administration."

In his email, Taylor pointed to his longstanding history of bi-partisanship and mentioned he had been a big supporter of Hillary Clinton's quest for the presidency.

SHRM members have criticized Taylor, accusing him of giving in to the political right's "call to destroy equity" and kowtowing to businesses instead of representing both businesses and people. Others have referred to SHRM more as a lobbyist than an organization for the development of the HR profession.

Allison Mairena Sproul, Global Vice President of People at NewGlobe directed her comment to Taylor, saying, "The most important non-negotiable I want to see from SHRM is the removal of you from the CEO position. It's clear you do not represent the interests of today's HR leaders."

In response to the accusations that SHRM's decision was kowtowing to political pressures, Taylor wrote, "We acknowledge that there are groups wanting to eliminate all DEI (not just equity). Their motivations for wanting it eliminated vary, but it didn't factor at all into our decision-making. If we wanted to make the far right happy, we'd stop using DEI entirely. Instead, we know there is incredible work to do in this space, and we will proudly lead with Inclusion & Diversity while acknowledging any successful Inclusion strategy will necessarily incorporate principles of accessibility, equity, belonging and civility."

Where Does This Leave DEI?

Equity has long been a rallying cry for a host of *othered* groups who argue that companies can have diversity and even invite people to sit at the table. But if those people don't have a voice, then it's tokenism.

Taylor says he isn't trying to change how other companies define this work and encourages them to keep DEI if it works for them. However, he does challenge HR practitioners to consider SHRM's rationale for a revised strategy.

"[Equity] is such a tough term, some people are going to immediately shut down just at the mention of it," Taylor told Kreigel. "If that's the case, and if you're genuinely committed to this work, are you willing to sort of die on the sword for the E? We're saying we're going to get the E but we're going to focus on the I and the D."

Taylor admits his biggest fear is that the decision could be wrong and that his 14-year-old might be having the same conversation 30 years from now. But he has high hopes and believes that the data-backed decision will yield encouraging results. Only time will tell.

5 – The Dangers of Forced Conformity in Diversity, Equity & Inclusion

Credit: Global Watchdog.

This chapter is from the Alan Wood "DEI Exposed: The Dangers of Forced Conformity in Diversity Equity & Inclusion" Global Watchdog March 2024 article:

Musings of an unabashed and unapologetic liberal deep in the heart of a Red State. Crusader against obscurantism. Optimistic curmudgeon, snark jockey, lovably opinionated purveyor of wisdom and truth. Multi-lingual world traveler and part-time irreverent philosopher who dabbles in writing, political analysis, and social commentary. Attempting to provide some sanity and clarity to complex issues with a dash of sardonic wit and humor. Thanks for visiting!

Beyond the Buzzwords: Unveiling the Dark Side of DEI

The mantra of Diversity, Equity, and Inclusion (DEI) has pervaded our workplaces, posing as a beacon of progress and inclusivity. Yet, beneath this polished veneer, there lies a troubling reality: systemic barriers remain entrenched, minority voices are drowned out, and a sense of disillusionment spreads like wildfire across both majority and minority groups. This stark contradiction between the lofty ideals and the sobering reality of DEI demands a rigorous, unflinching examination.

Our journey through this article is not merely academic. We are here to unravel the intricate web of economic, legal, psychological, and ethical threads that DEI initiatives weave, often to their own detriment. While the pursuit of inclusivity is noble, the path trodden by current DEI programs is fraught with pitfalls and paradoxes, leading us astray from our shared goal of a truly inclusive society.

In this critical exploration, we will lay bare the hidden dangers of DEI, dissecting its economic, legal, and psychological implications, and challenging the often-unquestioned assumptions it carries. Our aim is not to dismantle the desire for positive change but to shine a light on the chasm between aspiration and reality, igniting a necessary dialogue for genuine, effective inclusivity.

Our analysis is not just an academic exercise; it's a call to action. We stand at a crossroads, where the choice is ours to either continue down a path of superficial gestures or to pave a new way forward, rooted in substance, critical thinking, and true inclusivity. Join us as we delve into the complexities of DEI, not to dwell on its flaws but to forge a path toward a future where diversity is not just a buzzword, but a lived reality.

Through this comprehensive analysis, we will:

- **Expose the potential pitfalls and unintended consequences of current DEI initiatives.**

- **Explore the economic, legal, psychological, and ethical implications of DEI programs.**

- **Challenge the assumptions often associated with DEI and offer alternative perspectives.**

- **Promote a more nuanced and data-driven approach to fostering genuine inclusivity.**

- **Ultimately, ignite a call to action for a recalibration of DEI efforts, ensuring they align with their true purpose.**

This journey into the complexities of DEI is not about dwelling on the shortcomings of the present, but rather about laying the groundwork for a more equitable and inclusive future. It is a call for collective action, a shared responsibility to bridge the gap between intention and impact, and a commitment to building a world where diversity is not just celebrated, but truly lived and experienced by all.

Historical Context: Unveiling the Dark Side of DEI

Initially conceived as a beacon of hope against historical inequalities, DEI initiatives in academia promised inclusive environments where marginalized voices could resonate. However, the trajectory of these initiatives has veered sharply, morphing into ideological battlegrounds, as aptly observed by Fareed Zakaria. Universities, once the bastions of intellectual freedom, now find themselves ensnared in a web of ideological conformity, often at the behest of DEI advocates.

The University of Chicago's Kalven Report, a seminal document underscoring the importance of ideological neutrality in academia, seems a distant memory in today's DEI landscape. The report's call for academic freedom and open inquiry stands in stark contrast to the current state of affairs, where dissenting voices are stifled, and ideological alignment is often enforced.

This ideological drift in DEI initiatives is not just a matter of academic concern; it reflects a broader societal shift. What began as an earnest effort to rectify past injustices has, in some cases, evolved into a tool for enforcing conformity. This trend raises alarm bells, signaling a need for urgent reform to reclaim the original vision of DEI—one that truly fosters diversity of thought and promotes a pluralistic society.

Legal Risks and Compliance Challenges in DEI Programs

The legal landscape surrounding Diversity, Equity, and Inclusion (DEI) initiatives presents a complex and often overlooked aspect of these programs. As highlighted in the Reuters article by Sarah E. Fortt, Danielle Conley, and Nineveh Alkhas, "Diversity matters: the four scary legal risks hiding in your DEI program," DEI initiatives, while well-intentioned, can inadvertently lead to significant legal challenges. The authors caution, "In the rush to implement DEI initiatives, many companies overlook the importance of legal oversight, leading to potential legal actions against them."

One of the primary legal risks associated with DEI programs is non-compliance with existing anti-discrimination laws. While aiming to foster diversity, these initiatives can sometimes inadvertently create scenarios where discrimination occurs in reverse—favoring one group over another based on characteristics such as race, gender, or ethnicity. This can lead to legal challenges, as the authors note: "DEI goals, especially when poorly framed, can sometimes clash with the legal framework designed to prevent discrimination."

Moreover, the implementation of DEI programs often lacks a comprehensive understanding of regulatory requirements, leading to a mismatch between the initiatives and the legal framework within which organizations operate. This gap can expose organizations to legal risks, as Fortt, Conley, and Alkhas warn, "Failure to consider all stakeholders and regulatory requirements can lead to initiatives that are more harmful than helpful."

Another article, "7 Ways Your DEI Initiatives Are Harming Your Company and How To Resolve It" by Brian Dapelo, echoes similar concerns, highlighting how DEI programs can inadvertently lead to workplace discrimination. Dapelo states, "In their quest for diversity, some organizations end up discriminating in the name of inclusion, paradoxically undermining the very principles DEI stands for."

Furthermore, DEI initiatives sometimes lack sufficient legal support, particularly for DEI officers tasked with implementing these programs. This oversight can result in a disjointed approach that fails to align DEI efforts with legal and regulatory standards, as noted in the Reuters article: "Insufficient legal support for DEI officers can lead to initiatives that are legally unsound and potentially damaging."

These legal and compliance challenges underscore the necessity for a more cautious and legally informed approach to DEI initiatives. As organizations strive to create inclusive environments, they must navigate the complex legal landscape with care, ensuring that their efforts to promote diversity do not inadvertently lead to new forms of discrimination or legal entanglements.

Effectiveness and Counterproductivity of DEI Training

The effectiveness and potential counterproductivity of Diversity, Equity, and Inclusion (DEI) training programs have been a subject of intense debate. Rod Dreher, in his article "DEI Training: Harmful, Phony, And Expensive" published by The American Conservative, presents a critical view, arguing that these programs are costly, ineffective, and may even reinforce biases. He cites research suggesting that "DEI training is a high-cost endeavor with little evidence of long-term effectiveness."

Dreher further criticizes the approach of DEI training, often seen as performative rather than transformative. He notes that "instead of fostering genuine understanding, DEI training can provoke backlash and deepen divisions." This sentiment resonates with other critiques questioning the focus on personal belief changes, a strategy deemed both intrusive and ineffective. The simplistic view of complex social dynamics adopted by some DEI training programs is also highlighted as problematic. As Dreher points out, "DEI training oversimplifies the complexities of human behavior and interaction, leading to superficial solutions to deep-rooted problems."

These criticisms raise concerns about a potential disconnect between the goals of DEI training and its real-world impact. Instead of fostering inclusivity and understanding, some programs may actually contribute to division and skepticism about their value and efficacy.

Misguided Focus and Unintended Outcomes of DEI Initiatives

While intended to promote workplace and societal harmony, Diversity, Equity, and Inclusion (DEI) initiatives can ironically lead to various unintended and adverse consequences. This section draws on Brian Dapelo's analysis in "7 Ways Your DEI Initiatives Are Harming Your Company and How To Resolve It," which outlines several critical concerns.

Dapelo highlights the potential for DEI efforts to inadvertently promote discrimination. He argues that "flawed execution can result in favoring certain groups over others, contradicting the principles of equality and fairness." This can create resentment and undermine the very goals of DEI initiatives.

Furthermore, the overemphasis on physical attributes in some DEI programs, instead of focusing on individual qualities and merit, is another concern. Dapelo warns that "such practices can diminish the overall talent pool and decrease performance by prioritizing external characteristics over skills and experience." This not only undermines meritocratic principles but can also foster divisiveness within organizations.

Additionally, attributing individual accomplishments to demographic factors rather than personal merit can be demotivating and counterproductive. Dapelo observes that "such practices can belittle individual achievements, creating a workplace culture that prioritizes labels over individual contributions."

Finally, the potential for DEI initiatives to distract from core organizational goals is another critical point. Dapelo notes that "an excessive focus on DEI can lead to a dilution of focus and resources, hindering the achievement of primary objectives."

These critiques raise serious questions about the effectiveness of conventional DEI approaches. While the intentions behind such programs are often commendable, their implementation can lead to outcomes that are directly counterproductive to the goals of fairness and inclusivity. The following section will delve deeper into the systemic issues associated with these conventional approaches and explore alternative solutions.

Systemic Issues and Superficial Approaches in Conventional DEI Initiatives

While Diversity, Equity, and Inclusion (DEI) initiatives are intended to create inclusive environments and address historical inequalities, they often face criticism for their systemic issues and superficial approaches. Dr. Ted Sun, in his article "Dangers of the Conventional DEI Initiatives," published by Transcontinental University, delves into these concerns.

Sun argues that traditional DEI training can be ineffective and even harmful. He describes a "blame game" within such programs, which fails to foster genuine understanding or lasting change. Furthermore, he criticizes quota-driven approaches, a common feature in DEI initiatives, suggesting that they prioritize superficial diversity without addressing underlying biases or building meaningful relationships across diverse groups.

Sun advocates for a shift towards a values-based systemic approach to DEI. This approach emphasizes core values awareness and leadership development, aiming to move beyond the limitations of quotas and training. By addressing unconscious bias at a deeper level, it seeks to create lasting change and build a truly inclusive culture. Sun warns that without a values-driven foundation, DEI initiatives risk becoming counterproductive, exacerbating the very divisions they are meant to bridge.

This critique emphasizes the need for a more holistic and value-centric approach to diversity and inclusion. One that goes beyond superficial measures and integrates into the very fabric of organizational culture, promoting genuine understanding and respect for all individuals.

Comprehensive Analysis and Case Studies on the Dangers of DEI Initiatives

This section delves into the dangers of Diversity, Equity, and Inclusion (DEI) initiatives through a series of case studies and expanded critiques, providing a comprehensive picture of the challenges these programs often encounter.

Case Study 1: Impingement on Free Speech and Open Debate

In Fareed Zakaria's article, he details a case from a U.S. university where events organized by Students for Justice in Palestine were disrupted. This incident illustrates how DEI efforts, despite good intentions, can inadvertently stifle free speech and open debate in academic settings. The delicate balance between promoting inclusivity and preserving the bedrock principles of academic freedom and dialogue is a challenge DEI initiatives often struggle to navigate.

Case Study 2: Legal Ramifications and Reverse Discrimination

An article from Reuters discusses a situation where a corporate DEI initiative led to a lawsuit alleging reverse discrimination. This example highlights the potential legal risks associated with DEI programs and emphasizes the need for meticulous legal oversight in their implementation. Balancing the goal of fostering diversity and inclusion with adhering to legal and ethical standards presents a significant challenge for organizations.

Case Study 3: Unintended Reinforcement of Biases

Rod Dreher critiques corporate DEI training in his article, highlighting a case where training sessions inadvertently reinforced existing biases rather than diminishing them. This demonstrates the potential for DEI training to backfire, exacerbating the very problems it seeks to resolve and heightening workplace tensions.

Case Study 4: Decreased Performance and Increased Divisiveness

Brian Dapelo analyzes a company where DEI initiatives led to decreased overall performance and increased employee divisiveness. This example illustrates the potential for poorly managed DEI efforts to be counterproductive, dividing the workforce instead of unifying it.

Case Study 5: Superficial Diversity Efforts

Dr. Ted Sun's analysis focuses on an organization that prioritized meeting diversity quotas without addressing underlying systemic issues. This well-intentioned approach resulted in a veneer of diversity that failed to create a truly inclusive or equitable environment. It serves as a reminder that DEI initiatives must delve beyond superficial changes to effect real, systemic transformation.

Beyond Specific Examples: Broader Considerations

In addition to these specific cases, we also explore the broader impacts of DEI initiatives, including their psychological effects on individuals, economic implications for organizations, and long-term efficacy in achieving societal change. The global dimension of DEI is also considered, emphasizing the need for culturally nuanced approaches. This analysis of DEI initiatives, through diverse perspectives and real-world examples, highlights the complexity of these programs and the multifaceted challenges they face. By acknowledging these challenges and implementing thoughtful, nuanced, and well-executed strategies, DEI can contribute positively to organizations and society as a whole.

Alternative Approaches and Solutions

In light of the limitations of conventional Diversity, Equity, and Inclusion (DEI) initiatives, exploring alternative approaches that foster genuine inclusivity and effectiveness becomes crucial. This section delves into several promising solutions.

Values-Based Systemic Approach:

Dr. Ted Sun proposes a critical shift from quota-driven methods to a values-based systemic approach. This approach prioritizes integrating core values and leadership development into DEI strategies, aiming to address unconscious bias and build authentic relationships within organizations. This shift fosters a culture of inclusivity and respect, rather than solely focusing on numerical representation.

Promoting Inclusive Actions and Behaviors:

Instead of attempting to change personal beliefs, a more practical and effective approach focuses on promoting inclusive actions and behaviors. This involves creating environments where diverse perspectives are not only included but also valued and respected, nurturing a genuinely inclusive atmosphere where everyone feels comfortable contributing their unique experiences and perspectives.

Legal and Compliance Integration:

Ensuring that DEI initiatives comply with legal and ethical standards is crucial. This necessitates close collaboration with legal teams to design programs that adhere to anti-discrimination laws and other relevant regulations. By prioritizing legal and ethical compliance, organizations can safeguard themselves against potential legal pitfalls while promoting fairness and equity.

Cultural Competence Training:

Generic DEI training often falls short, failing to address the nuances of cultural differences. Culturally competent training, however, focuses on enhancing understanding and respect for diverse cultural backgrounds. This becomes especially crucial in a globalized workforce where cultural misunderstandings can lead to conflict and exclusion. Cultivating cultural competence is essential for building a truly inclusive environment.

Long-Term Commitment and Continuous Evaluation:

Viewing DEI initiatives as a long-term commitment rather than a one-off effort is vital for their success. Regularly measuring the impact and effectiveness of these programs through surveys, data analysis, and feedback mechanisms is essential to ensure they are achieving their intended goals and making a real difference. This commitment to ongoing evaluation and improvement underscores the importance of sustainability and adaptability in DEI initiatives.

By adopting these alternative approaches, organizations and institutions can create DEI initiatives that are legally sound, ethically robust, and truly effective in fostering diversity, equity, and inclusion. A strategic shift towards values-driven, culturally competent, and adaptable DEI strategies is imperative for realizing the full potential of diversity in our society.

Equity vs. Equality in DEI Initiatives

A critical analysis of Diversity, Equity, and Inclusion (DEI) initiatives reveals a crucial distinction between two key concepts: equity and equality. While often used interchangeably, these terms have vastly different implications for DEI efforts.

Defining the Difference:

- **Equality:** Providing every individual with the same resources and opportunities, regardless of their background or circumstances.

- **Equity:** Recognizing and addressing the individual and systemic challenges faced by different groups, ensuring everyone has equal opportunities to succeed.

The Pitfalls of Overemphasizing Equality:

Many DEI initiatives prioritize treating everyone the same, overlooking the unique needs and barriers faced by diverse groups. This approach falls short by failing to address the root causes of inequality. For example, offering identical training to all employees ignores the fact that some may require additional support or specialized resources to overcome systemic hurdles.

The Necessity of Equity-Focused DEI Initiatives:

True inclusivity necessitates a shift towards equity-focused DEI strategies. This requires acknowledging and addressing the individual and systemic challenges faced by different groups. Examples of equity-focused strategies include:

- **Targeted mentoring programs:** Supporting underrepresented groups through mentorship programs tailored to their specific needs.

- **Adjusted recruitment strategies:** Reaching a broader pool of candidates by diversifying recruitment channels and removing biased practices.

- **Accessibility measures:** Making the workplace accessible and inclusive for individuals with disabilities.

- **Culturally competent leadership:** Developing leaders who are aware of and sensitive to cultural differences.

Case Study: The Tech Industry and the Need for Equity:

The tech industry provides a compelling case study. Despite efforts to promote diversity, many underrepresented groups continue to face unique challenges that are not addressed by a one-size-fits-all approach. An equity-focused strategy, acknowledging the specific barriers faced by each group, is crucial for achieving lasting change.

Implementing Effective Equity Strategies:

Effective equity strategies require:

- **Deep understanding:** Engaging in continuous dialogue and listening to the needs of various groups.

- **Regular assessment:** Evaluating the effectiveness of current DEI strategies and identifying areas for improvement.

- **Adaptability:** Responding to feedback and adjusting strategies based on changing circumstances.

Shifting the focus from equality to equity is essential for achieving the true goals of DEI initiatives. By understanding the different needs of diverse groups and implementing tailored strategies to address them, DEI initiatives can create truly inclusive environments where everyone has the opportunity to thrive.

The Economic Dimension of DEI: Misallocation and Inefficiency

While Diversity, Equity, and Inclusion (DEI) initiatives have gained momentum, their economic impact deserves closer examination. This section explores the potential for misallocation of resources and inefficiencies within DEI programs, raising questions about their cost-effectiveness and overall impact.

Resource Allocation and Return on Investment:

A significant concern is whether the substantial financial resources directed towards DEI initiatives are translating into proportional benefits. A critical assessment of the return on investment (ROI) is needed, focusing on tangible improvements in workplace diversity, productivity, and overall organizational well-being.

Efficiency in Achieving Desired Outcomes:

The efficiency of DEI initiatives is often questioned. While significant funds are allocated to workshops, training programs, and various other activities, the effectiveness of these expenditures in achieving desired outcomes like inclusivity and equitable opportunities remains unclear. This raises the need to identify more efficient means of utilizing these resources.

Economic Impact of Misguided DEI Efforts:

Misguided or poorly implemented DEI programs can have unintended negative economic consequences. For example, initiatives that inadvertently lead to a divided workforce, reduced morale, or even legal challenges can result in significant financial losses for organizations.

Strategic and Targeted DEI Investments:

To enhance the effectiveness of DEI initiatives, a more strategic and targeted approach to resource allocation is crucial. This involves prioritizing key areas for investment, implementing evidence-based practices, and continuously evaluating the effectiveness of these interventions.

Incorporating Economic Analysis in DEI Planning:

Thorough economic analysis should be incorporated into the planning and execution of DEI initiatives. This involves setting clear, measurable goals, assessing the cost-effectiveness of different strategies, and regularly evaluating progress towards achieving these goals.

Ensuring the economic viability and effectiveness of DEI initiatives requires a strategic and data-driven approach. By prioritizing impactful interventions, utilizing resources efficiently, and continuously evaluating progress, DEI programs can achieve meaningful and sustainable progress towards diversity, equity, and inclusion while maintaining economic viability.

Cult-Like Behavior and Intellectual Stifling in DEI Initiatives

The implementation of Diversity, Equity, and Inclusion (DEI) initiatives has, in some cases, exhibited concerning trends that resemble cult-like behavior and intellectual restriction. This section explores how these issues can manifest and the negative consequences they have on open discourse and intellectual diversity.

Suppression of Dissent: A worrying trend is the suppression of dissenting voices that challenge the prevailing DEI narrative. The case of Professor Dorian Abbot at MIT, whose lecture was canceled due to his views on DEI, exemplifies this issue. Such incidents highlight how certain DEI environments become echo chambers, intolerant of diverse perspectives.

Cultish Monomania: In some cases, DEI efforts exhibit a "cultish monomania," where promoting diversity morphs into enforcing a singular, unquestionable set of beliefs. This creates an environment where any association with ideas deemed incompatible with the DEI agenda is deemed "impure" and leads to exclusion or censure.

Impact on Intellectual Discourse: This monolithic approach stifles intellectual exploration and debate. In academic settings, where diverse viewpoints and critical thinking are crucial, this trend poses a significant threat to intellectual rigor and discovery.

Monoculture of Thought: The cult-like adherence to specific DEI doctrines risks creating a monoculture of thought, where dissenting voices are not just discouraged but actively silenced. This undermines the very goals of

DEI, which aim to foster inclusivity and respect for diverse perspectives.

Need for Balance: To avoid these pitfalls, a more balanced and inclusive approach is necessary. This includes creating spaces for open and respectful dialogue, where differing opinions are welcome and valued as essential components of a truly inclusive environment. DEI initiatives must resist the temptation to become dogmatic and remain open to a plurality of perspectives to be truly effective and uphold their integrity. Only through such a balanced approach can DEI foster environments that are both inclusive and intellectually vibrant.

The Illiberal Nature of DEI Initiatives

Despite their intended goals of promoting diversity and inclusion, some Diversity, Equity, and Inclusion (DEI) initiatives have been criticized for their illiberal nature, particularly concerning intellectual freedom and diversity of thought. This section examines how, paradoxically, DEI efforts can stifle dissent and create environments intolerant of differing viewpoints.

Conformity over Diversity of Thought: One key criticism is the prioritization of ideological conformity over genuine diversity of thought. This concern extends from academic institutions to corporate settings, where individuals might feel pressured to conform to specific beliefs promoted by DEI programs.

Stifling Academic and Intellectual Freedom: The potential threat to academic freedom and open discourse is particularly concerning in educational institutions. DEI initiatives that penalize individuals for holding dissenting views can significantly hinder intellectual exploration and discovery.

Creating Intellectual Echo Chambers: By fostering environments where only certain viewpoints are tolerated, DEI initiatives risk creating intellectual echo chambers. This can stifle creativity and innovation, ultimately undermining the very diversity and inclusivity these programs aim to achieve.

Balancing DEI with Intellectual Diversity: Finding the right balance between DEI goals and intellectual diversity is crucial. Effective DEI initiatives should create spaces where diverse perspectives are welcomed, encouraged, and engaged with in a respectful and constructive manner.

Encouraging Open Dialogue and Debate: Open dialogue and debate are essential for fostering a truly inclusive environment. DEI programs should provide platforms for diverse opinions to be shared and discussed without fear of retribution. This not only enriches the discourse but also promotes understanding and inclusivity. While the intentions of DEI initiatives are commendable, it is crucial to ensure that they do not become counterproductive by stifling intellectual freedom and diversity of thought. A balanced and open approach is essential for DEI initiatives to truly foster inclusive environments that embrace a broad spectrum of perspectives.

Conclusion: A Call for Recalibration and Responsible DEI

This comprehensive analysis has exposed the potential pitfalls and unintended consequences of current Diversity, Equity, and Inclusion (DEI) initiatives. While the pursuit of inclusivity is undeniably noble, the current approach, with its emphasis on superficiality, conformity, and ideological adherence, poses serious threats to fundamental freedoms and societal cohesion.

The evidence presented throughout this analysis paints a sobering picture:

- **Impingement on Free Speech and Open Debate:** DEI initiatives can inadvertently stifle open dialogue and critical discourse, creating environments of intellectual conformity.

- **Legal Ramifications and Reverse Discrimination:** Poorly designed DEI programs can lead to legal challenges and unintended consequences, undermining the very principles of fairness and equity they aim to promote.

- **Unintended Reinforcement of Biases:** Generic DEI training may inadvertently reinforce existing biases instead of dismantling them, further exacerbating societal divisions.

- **Superficial Diversity Efforts:** Focusing on quotas and superficial changes without addressing underlying systemic issues fails to create genuine inclusivity and perpetuates the feeling of tokenism.

- **Economic Misallocation and Inefficiency:** The substantial resources allocated to DEI initiatives may not be yielding proportional benefits, raising concerns about the economic viability and effectiveness of these programs.

Therefore, a call for mere reform is insufficient. A fundamental reevaluation of the entire DEI paradigm is essential. This requires a shift from:

- **Superficiality to substance:** Moving beyond tokenism and quotas to address underlying systemic issues that perpetuate inequality.

- **Conformity to diversity of thought:** Encouraging open dialogue, critical thinking, and the acceptance of diverse viewpoints.

- **Ideological adherence to merit:** Focusing on individual merit and potential rather than enforcing a specific set of beliefs.

- **Economic inefficiency to effectiveness:** Implementing cost-effective and evidence-based strategies that maximize the impact of DEI initiatives.

This recalibration of DEI efforts necessitates:

- **Critical assessment of existing initiatives:** Evaluating the effectiveness of current programs and identifying areas for improvement.

- **Development of data-driven approaches:** Utilizing evidence-based practices and setting clear, measurable goals to track progress.

- **Transparency and accountability:** Ensuring transparency in the implementation of DEI initiatives and holding organizations accountable for their outcomes.

- **Continuous dialogue and feedback:** Fostering open communication and actively seeking feedback from diverse stakeholders.

Ultimately, the goal is to create a society that embraces genuine inclusivity, respects individual dignity, and upholds the core values of equality, freedom, and meritocracy. This requires a collective effort from individuals, institutions, and organizations to move beyond the current flawed DEI paradigm and build a future where diversity is truly valued and celebrated in all its forms.

6 – Keeping Your Corporation Out of the DEI Culture War

Credit: Vivek Ramaswamy, partial cover image from his book Woke, Inc.

A new Pew Research Center survey conducted by Rachel Minkin titled "Views of DEI Have Become Slightly More Negative Among U.S. Workers" in November 2024 American workers' opinions on the role of diversity, equity and inclusion efforts in the workplace have become more negative since last year.

Compared with February 2023, workers are now somewhat more likely to say:

- Focusing on increasing DEI at work is mainly a bad thing.

- Their company or organization pays too much attention to increasing DEI.

In a separate survey, we asked Americans overall—regardless of their employment status—about their views on the impact of DEI practices in the workplace.

- More Americans say DEI practices help rather than hurt Black, Hispanic and Asian men and women, as well as White women.

- In turn, far more Americans say DEI hurts White men than say it helps them (36% vs. 14%).

These findings come from two recent surveys: one conducted among U.S. workers in October 2024 and another among U.S. adults in September 2024. Additional findings come from a previous Center survey of U.S. workers conducted in February 2023.

Views of DEI Have Become Slightly More Negative Among U.S. Workers

About half of workers (52%) now say focusing on increasing DEI at work is mainly a good thing, down from 56% in February 2023. The share of workers who say this is a bad thing (21%) is up 5 percentage points since last year. About a quarter (26%) say focusing on DEI is neither good nor bad.

As was the case in 2023, women, Democrats, and Black, Hispanic and Asian workers are among the groups most likely to say focusing on increasing DEI in the workplace is a good thing.

Republicans and men continue to be among the groups of workers most likely to see DEI efforts as a bad thing, and their views have become more negative since last year.

About four-in-ten Republican and Republican-leaning workers (42%) now say focusing on DEI is a bad thing, up from 30% last year. The share of Republicans who offer a neutral view has dropped 8 points, while the share who see it as a good thing is virtually unchanged.

Among employed men, 29% say focusing on DEI is a bad thing, up from 23% who said this in February 2023. The share of male workers who see this as a good thing has dropped 6 points, from 50% in 2023 to 44% today.

Asian workers have also become less likely since 2023 to see DEI efforts as a good thing: 57% of Asian workers say this, down from 72%. More Asian workers now offer a neutral view of DEI than did so last year. About three-in-ten (28%) now say focusing on DEI is neither good nor bad, compared with 18% in 2023.

There has been little change in views of DEI as a good thing among White and Black workers. However, among White workers, a growing share say DEI is a bad thing: 27% say this today, up from 21% in 2023.

Workers' views on the attention paid to DEI in the workplace

About half of workers overall (52%) say their company or organization pays about the right amount of attention to increasing DEI. That share has remained fairly stable since last year.

But a growing share of workers say their company pays too much attention to increasing DEI. In February 2023, workers were about as likely to say their company or organization pays too much attention to DEI as they were to say it paid too little attention (14% vs. 15%). Today, more say their workplace pays too much than too little attention (19% vs. 12%).

Views by race and ethnicity

White, Black and Hispanic workers are now slightly more likely to say their company or organization pays too much attention to increasing DEI than they were in 2023.

Today, 8% of Black workers say their company or organization pays too much attention to DEI, up from 3% in February 2023. In turn, 18% now say their company or organization pays too little attention to DEI, down from 28% in 2023.

The views of Asian workers on whether their company or organization pays too much or too little attention to DEI have not changed significantly since 2023.

Views by party

Republicans and Democrats are both more likely than in 2023 to say their company pays too much attention to increasing DEI:

- 29% of Republicans and Republican-leaning independents say this today, up from 24% in 2023.

- 10% of Democrats and Democratic leaners say this, up from 6%.

At the same time, the share of Democratic workers who say their company pays too little attention to DEI has dropped 5 points, from 21% to 16%. There has been no change in this view among Republican workers.

Americans' views of the impact of DEI practices in the workplace

We separately asked Americans, regardless of their employment status, to weigh in on DEI practices in the workplace and whether these efforts help or hurt certain groups.

More Americans say DEI practices help Black, Hispanic and Asian men and women than say DEI hurts them.

Opinions are more mixed about the impact on White women in the workplace. Three-in-ten Americans say DEI practices help White women, compared with 23% who say they hurt them.

In contrast, far more say DEI practices hurt White men than help them (36% vs. 14%).

For the most part, similar shares of men and women say DEI practices help each group. But by margins of 4 to 16 points, men are more likely than women to say these practices hurt each group. For example, 45% of men say DEI practices hurt White men in the workplace, compared with 29% of women who say the same.

Views by race and ethnicity

White and Asian adults are especially likely to say DEI practices help various groups—including Black women and men, Hispanic women and men, and Asian women. In turn, Black and Hispanic adults (29% and 23%) are more likely than other groups to say DEI practices help White men in the workplace.

White adults are more likely than other racial and ethnic groups to say DEI practices hurt White men and women in the workplace:

- 47% of White adults say DEI practices in the workplace hurt White men.

- 29% of White adults say DEI practices hurt White women.

This is much higher than the shares of Black, Hispanic and Asian adults who say the same about the impact of DEI on White men and women.

Views by party

Republicans and Democrats are both more likely to say DEI practices help than hurt Black, Hispanic and Asian men and women. But Republicans are more likely than Democrats to say these practices hurt all of the groups asked about in the survey. In turn, Democrats are more likely than Republicans to say they help each group.

These differences are especially evident in views of the impact of DEI on White men. A 56% majority of Republicans say DEI practices hurt White men, compared with 19% of Democrats—a difference of 37 percentage points.

7 Metrics to Measure Your Organization's DEI Progress

Is your organization a true meritocracy? This is an ideal most leaders aspire to but few have the data to back those assertions up. To assess progress, you should track seven key metrics that span the entire employee life cycle as outlined in the May 2023 Lee Jourdan "7 Metrics to Measure Your Organization's DEI Progress" in the *Harvard Business Review*.

Most leaders agree in theory that people should be given opportunities for development and promotion based on merit. But how can any organization ensure that's actually happening in practice? Employing the right metrics to benchmark and track are key to achieving a merit-based culture.

In my three decades of experience as an executive in the energy industry and now as an independent board director and advisor in tech and human capital management, I've found seven metrics—spanning the entire employee life cycle—to be most useful for assessing progress towards a true meritocracy.

1. Attrition
2. Performance
3. Promotions
4. Leadership Pipeline
5. Employment Pipeline

6. Pay Equity
7. Inclusion

You might notice that the first letters spell "apple pie" minus the "e." That's so it's easy to remember and, since "pi" is a number, to enforce the quantitative nature of this exercise.

Note that within each metric, I'd expect companies to track various employee cohorts: differentiated as allowed by law, region, and culture. In the United States, that is, race, gender, ethnicity, and where appropriate other dimensions of diversity such as sexual orientation and veteran status.

Here's a deeper dive into the data you'll want to consider in each category.

Attrition

There are two subsets to attrition: voluntary and involuntary. So, you'll want to track whether or not you are disproportionately losing or letting go of people from underrepresented groups. On the involuntary front, this includes testing for "adverse impact," which U.S. law defines as "employment practices that appear neutral but have a discriminatory effect on a protected group."

You'll also want to track voluntary attrition to see if it's as common among majority group employees as it is among underrepresented group employees. Or if it differs between the different underrepresented groups. This should include not only collecting hard data, and comparing it against your own and national averages, but also conducting exit interviews with all departing employees to figure out why they're leaving and whether bias or not feeling included had anything to do with it.

The U.S department of Labor's Bureau of Labor Statistics provides attrition rates by industry for the US. In the UK, it's the Office for National Statistics. These sources can help organizations benchmark and establish whether attrition is an area of opportunity to address. Attrition is a lagging indicator, meaning you don't know you have a problem until after the fact, but it can be a red flag—a warning sign that systemic bias exists.

Performance

63% of corporations still use an annual performance review process, and most assign a letter or a number to each employee. A process I refer to as subjective objectivity because the assignation of a score often fools us into believing that it's based on fact not opinion.

Here, you're looking for equal distribution of high and low ratings across all groups. For example, if one group is receiving a higher share of low ratings than their overall representation, or another group is receiving a higher share of high ratings than their overall representation indicates they should, this could be a sign of bias in the process.

Low performance ratings for a specific group over time could reveal bias not just in reviews about also access to opportunities to outperform. Performance results should be reviewed at the overall organization level, but also at the functional level such as within finance and sales. Performance ratings can be a leading indicator of promotion outcomes. If this is the case, consider not relying on performance ratings when considering promotions, but on competency either measured or observed and demonstrated results that meet or exceed expected outcomes.

Promotion

Promotion rates should be assessed by pay grade, race, and gender, and again assessed for balance between different demographic groups. Are promotion rates balanced at the entry and junior level, and then skewed in favor of the majority at higher levels? Are certain groups seeing high proportion rates for technical jobs, but not in leadership positions? The more granular the analysis, the more likely organizations will uncover bias. If organizations believe they have achieved meritocracy, promotion rates across gender and racial lines should be relatively balanced.

Transparency around promotions is the next step. For example, in the United States, Walmart shares promotion rates by race and gender in their annual Culture, Diversity, Equity, & Inclusion report, while Consolidated Edison shares it in their public DEI Annual Report over a five-year period. Joan Jacobs, VP learning and inclusion at the latter company, says "Transparency around DEI data is a way to lead by example. We are positioned to hold ourselves accountable to ensure our actions align with our words."

Leadership pipeline

Many organizations have established future leaders' programs. These are typically the top 2-3% of performers in each function further delineated by pay grade. They have been tapped as up-and-comers and given stretch assignments that allow them to shine so they typically develop leadership capabilities more quickly, putting them on an accelerated career trajectory. This pool of high performers becomes the most senior leadership cohort 10, 15, 20 years in the future. So, if your leadership pipeline is not diverse you've essentially locked in a non-diverse senior executive team for the future. Selection of future leaders includes performance and promotions, both of which are subject to bias.

An organization's leadership pipeline should reflect the representation of the workforce at a minimum but should also reflect what leadership will look like when diversity objectives are met. For example, if the goal is to have a C-Suite that is staffed with 45% women, then the leader pipeline should be 45% women. Succession plans and future leader programs should reflect the representation goals of the organization.

Employment pipeline

New hire diversity is an oft-used but lagging indicator of how your employment pipeline is working. We count heads as they come in the door. But that's the end of the hiring pipeline. The real work is done prior to that. For a more holistic view of the effectiveness of hiring practices, organizations should assess the entire pipeline, starting with applications, then interviews, offers, and acceptance rates.

Of those that apply, what percent of each affinity are offered interviews? Is that percentage the same regardless of race and gender? If for example, X percent of white males that apply receive interviews, are we seeing the same success rate for candidates of color and women? Of those that receive interviews, what percentage are receiving offers? Again, does this vary by gender and race? And lastly, of those that receive offers, what percentage accept the offer? Low acceptance rates from specific groups could be a red flag about company culture. What happened on the site visit? Did they see people that looked like them? Did they feel like they had a community?

Pay equity

"Pay equity" and "pay gap" are two different analyses. Pay equity exists when employees are receiving the same pay for the same work regardless of how individuals identify. Pay gap is the delta in average compensation between two groups regardless of the types of jobs that make up that average.

While pay gap is important from a societal perspective and may highlight how different cohorts have access to different careers, it includes many variables that are not controlled by hiring organizations such as education paths, personal career decisions, attraction to certain industries, and regional impact.

By contrast, the factors impacting pay equity such as starting salary, pay adjustment policies, and pay reviews, are almost always under the control of organizations. A common trap is to pay based on tenure as opposed to competency. Pay structure should be a function of performance.

Testing for pay equity and sharing the results and/or actions to address shortfalls is one of the quickest ways to build credibility and support claims of fair and equitable treatment of employees.

Third party vendors such as Factorial HR and Rework provide guidance to do this kind of analysis in house. However, bringing a third party in and then sharing the results provides an added layer of credibility.

Inclusion

If diversity is counting heads, inclusion is making sure every head counts. It's becoming much more common for organizations to try to measure the employee experience—including the strength of manager relationships, a sense of belonging to one's peer group, and access to influential networks—and thanks to the use of data analytics and behavior-based algorithms it's now evolving into more science than art.

Some organizations choose to add inclusion questions to more general HR surveys, using platforms like Qualtrics or Culture Amp, while others will use dedicated, algorithm driven DEI platforms such as Pulsely which not only measure how inclusion varies amongst different identities, but measure inclusive behaviors of supervisors and managers.

For example, SEI, a technology and investment solutions firm uses these algorithms to assess the equity of workplace experiences, while, Convergent, a renewable energy company, also leverages data science to assess the inclusion competence of their leaders, placing them at the forefront of inclusivity.

Which path your organization takes is a function of what you are seeking to accomplish and when. Some questions to consider:

- Are we ready to learn why employees feel they don't belong, or is it enough now to just understand which groups feel disenfranchised?

- Can we act on findings that show our supervisors lack inclusive behaviors?

- Am I using a platform that is flexible enough to evolve as the science evolves?

Are my inclusion metrics on par with my diversity metrics?

We know that what gets measured gets done. We also know that transparent data provides one version of the truth and helps organizations determine priorities. These seven metrics, once established and benchmarked, can provide an accountability framework to demonstrate the success of DEI programs. It is rare to find any organization currently utilizing all these metrics, but all should aspire to.

Social Justice Movements, Employee Political Activism, and Internal Conflict

An Interesting analysis by Jonathan Haidt and Greg Lukianoff "How To Keep Your Corporation Out of the Culture War" article in Persuasion in December 2021 shows that beginning around 2018, parts of the corporate world began to experience the same changes universities were experiencing around 2014 about internal issues they are having with recent hires.

Their research told us that corporate America's youngest employees show increased levels of anxiety, depression, and fragility; a tendency to turn ordinary conflicts between co-workers into major issues requiring the attention of the Human Resources Department; and greater insistence that the organization must share and express their personal political values related to social justice.

This makes sense once you realize that members of Gen Z began to arrive on campuses in 2013 and 2014—they spent four years within institutions that largely catered to their new needs and demands, and began to graduate from four-year colleges around 2017 or 2018.

A 2021 survey found that 48% of Gen Z respondents reported feeling stress all or most of the time, and the top source of worry among them was career prospects. As for the increased internal conflicts and tensions among employees, the title of a 2021 article on the front page of the business section of *The New York Times* sums it up well: "The 37-Year-Olds Are Afraid of the 23-Year-Olds Who Work for Them." Friction and punishment campaigns in the corporate world seem to be hyper charged by Slack and other internal company messaging platforms.

Social Media Can Create a PR Nightmare for Employers

But why would Gen Z have any meaningful influence on corporations during this turbulent period—2017 to 2020—when they had just arrived in the workplace and were present only in small numbers? The primary reason comes back, again, to social media. Gen Z is the first generation where a critical mass of young people grew up as social media natives (with a 2018 survey finding 97% on at least one social media platform). This allowed them to organize and mobilize in a way that was simply not available to previous generations.

A single employee who is adept at using social media can create a PR nightmare for employers, often leading to nearly instantaneous public capitulation accompanied by a formulaic apology. Social media played a key role in the ouster of James Bennet from The New York Times in the summer of 2020, when many *NYT* staffers tweeted that he "[put] Black @nytimes staff in danger" by running an op-ed by U.S. Senator Tom Cotton in favor of deploying military force during civil unrest—phrasing they were advised to use by their union due to the existence of employment protections for speech relating to workplace safety.

The Outside Influence of Gen Z in the Workforce

And social media isn't the only place Gen Z is willing to take on their co-workers. Human resources is a growing field with expanding influence in modern corporations. Both of us have been told by business leaders that their human resources departments are struggling to keep up with increased utilization of HR by Gen Zers.

One contributing factor we hypothesize is that Gen Zers graduating from modern colleges have carried with them an inclination to appeal to intermediary authority in solving conflicts—an inclination which is fostered in K-12 and continues in higher education through systems like Bias Response teams.

But despite these two advantages, we believe the main reason Gen Z wields more influence is because a critical mass of their Millennial bosses and managers are sympathetic to them. Unsurprisingly, for both generations, personal ethics plays a larger role in their decisions about where and how to work.

Five years ago, about three-quarters of Millennials said business was a force for good; at the time, Gen Z made up about five percent of the workforce. Today, Gen Z makes up about a quarter of the workforce, and fewer than half of Millennials say that business is a force for good—bringing them roughly in line with Gen Z.

Millennials Seem to Share Gen Z's Skepticism About Capitalism

Whether the convergence came about by Gen Z influencing Millennials or because both generations responded in similar ways to the avalanche of social unrest since 2017 is unclear. But either way, Millennials seem to share Gen Z's skepticism about capitalism, and many of them share a willingness to prioritize social causes over company goals.

Ever since they entered the corporate world in the early 2000s, some members of the Millennial generation (born 1982 to 1996) have pushed for being able to "bring their whole selves to work." Companies in the creative industries encouraged this shift, erasing boundaries between work life and private life. But as America became ever more politically polarized, the problem with this policy became evident: Some whole selves cannot tolerate working alongside other whole selves that have different political beliefs and voting patterns.

At the same time, the tech booms of the late 1990s and 2000s saw an increased passion for what Whole Foods co-founder and CEO John Mackey calls "conscious capitalism": a desire by founders and CEOs to take a more positive role in social and environmental causes. Both of us have great sympathy for this movement and have been enthusiastic proponents. But in recent years we have seen some significant drawbacks.

On an everyday level, the move towards corporate social justice and the expectation of company-wide solidarity with specific causes can lead to what has (controversially) been dubbed "cancel culture." One of its defining patterns is that employees face calls for discipline or termination for expressing non-conforming opinions, even when those opinions are expressed away from the workplace or with no hostile intent.

Given the tendency of the American culture war to poison ever more aspects of personal and professional life, we think that leaders of all institutions should closely consider the costs of allowing their organizational culture to become what can increasingly feel like just another extension of Twitter.

8 Steps to Prevent Ideological Pressure and Political Conformity in the Workplace

Further analysis by Jonathan Haidt and Greg Lukianoff "How To Keep Your Corporation Out of the Culture War" article in Persuasion in December 2021 summarizes that for companies that wish to hire talent of all political stripes, or to reduce the frequency of campaigns to fire employees for political nonconformity, we offer the following advice.

1. Expand your definition of diversity. While racial diversity and gender expression often dominate what people mean by diversity on campus, for a company trying to serve a diverse market in a fast-changing economic environment, having diversity of opinion, diversity of experience, and diversity of social class and geographic background can be even more important. In fact, the kind of diversity most often found to confer advantages on teams is not demographic diversity but rather diversity of perspectives on topics closely related to the task at hand. This includes both functional diversity (e.g., what roles people play in the company) and political diversity (at least when trying to find truth about politically controversial topics).

2. Reconsider what colleges you hire from. While elite colleges offer the promise of bright and hard-working employees, the problems we covered in our book are generally more severe at elite private colleges. You might want to consider hiring from large state schools, and ones from regions of the country other than the West Coast or Northeast. This will increase your diversity by social class and region, and it may help your organization avoid the elite college groupthink that seems to be damaging some organizations, potentially giving your organization a competitive advantage.

You might want to go still further and consider hiring people who have not attended college at all, if you can put in place standards that still guarantee hard-working employees with relevant skills. We believe that the numbers of bright, hard-working, and talented people choosing to skip college or to learn through a less traditional alternative will increase in the coming years, while the ability of elite college graduates to work well with those who do not share their beliefs will continue to decline.

3. Orientation. Be direct with candidates and new hires. If you decide that you want your organization to be politically neutral or self-consciously politically heterogeneous it's a good idea to say so in job postings, and to introduce that idea to employees from their very first day. For example, you could state: "Our company's culture is oriented toward success in our mission, which is [lay out business mission here]. We therefore do not take public stands on issues that are not central to our business mission. If you're not willing to work for such a company, or with people who disagree with you on some of your deepest beliefs, this might not be the right organization for you."

4. Have a talk with the human resources department. A lot of the problems we see off-campus derive from ever-expanding definitions of harassment and discrimination, some of which come from institutions like the Equal Employment Opportunity Commission. The role that human resources has in preventing sexual or racial harassment is very important, but, unfortunately, similar departments on campus have been misused in order to police the expression of political opinion and ideological non-conformity.

In *The Coddling of the American Mind* we discussed Manning and Campbell's idea of moral dependency—that is, the problem of younger people being accustomed to dealing with any difficult interpersonal relationship by appealing to an authority. This makes sense in situations when you're talking about children; when reaching adulthood, however, students and potential employees should be able to navigate social interactions (even unpleasant but not harassing ones) themselves. Make sure your human resources department understands that employees are expected to deal with each other and navigate a way of getting along, and that they should only come to human resources if it involves something more serious.

5. Survey employees to see if there's a problem. Conduct anonymous surveys to figure out if employees feel there's a problem with the overall culture and climate, particularly to find out if it is seen as being unwelcoming toward members of any demographic or political group. Don't rely on your impressions from social media, which are often wildly out of sync with the real distribution of opinions.

6. If a social media firestorm demands that you fire an employee, slow down. If you're in a situation where online mobs are demanding that you get rid of an employee, you have a problem. Sometimes the mob may actually have a point—maybe you have hired somebody who has done unforgivable things that damage your organization's reputation. However, if that is the case, it will still look that way in two weeks or a month. Have a process in place that slows things down and allows time for careful investigation and due process. Twitter firestorms lose energy quickly so even having just a mandatory two-week cooling off period can get you past the critical period.

7. Don't make firing a first or preferred punishment. If someone has shown extremely poor judgment but has otherwise been an exemplary employee, consider something short of firing. As a society we should revive the virtue of forgiveness, and learn to accept apologies again.

8. Ask yourself "where does this end?" If you have an employee who other employees want terminated, and you do terminate them, you have set a precedent for what counts as a fireable offense. Over time, that line tends to shift in one direction only. Eventually, you may be left only with employees who share a narrow ideology and a punitive orientation toward all but the most doctrinaire speech.

Conclusion

Many of the dynamics we described in *The Coddling of the American Mind*, which transformed college campuses beginning in 2014, are now spreading rapidly through the corporate world in the U.S. We expect that the other English speaking nations are only a few years behind us.

We predict that internal cross-generational conflicts are going to get much more intense as more of Gen Z joins the Millennial generation and brings its additional concerns about emotional safety and its focus on individual words into the everyday misunderstandings of workplace interactions. We hope that the lessons learned on campus will be helpful for all generations as they navigate this difficult transition.

7 – Merit, Excellence, and Intelligence (MEI) Alternatives

Credit: HR Morning.

President Donald Trump has taken swift and significant actions against Diversity, Equity, and Inclusion (DEI) programs since returning to the White House in January 2025. On his first day in office, January 20, Trump signed an Executive Order titled "Ending Radical And Wasteful Government DEI Programs And Preferencing".

This order directed all federal DEI staff to be placed on paid leave and eventually laid off as reported in the Jack Kelly "President Trump Shifts To 'Merit, Excellence And Intelligence' In The Workplace And Away From DEI" Forbes February 2025 article:

Trump has described DEI programs as "dangerous, demeaning, and immoral," asserting that they are inherently discriminatory. He vowed to "create a society that is blind to color and based on merit". The executive order specifically targeted practices associated with DEI, positioning them as contrary to US law.

Rolling Back DEI Initiatives and Starting MEI Programs

President Trump believes in a new approach to hiring and workplace matters. This emerging movement advocates for "Merit, Excellence, and Intelligence (MEI)," which emphasizes selecting candidates based solely on their qualifications, abilities and intelligence.

Proponents argue that MEI offers a more equitable and effective method for building high-performing teams, moving away from demographic considerations to focus exclusively on individual merit.

MEI serves as a framework for making hiring decisions in the workplace. The aim is to choose job applicants based primarily on their achievements, skills, and contributions as opposed to other factors such as identity or demographic characteristics. MEI highlights the pursuit of the highest standards of performance in a person's occupation. A value is placed on tangible traits like problem-solving skills, inherent talent, and a high level of intelligence.

A number of companies have recently rolled back their DEI programs in favor of MEI initiatives, including Meta, McDonald's, Walmart, Ford, Harley-Davidson, John Deere, Tractor Supply Company, Amazon, and Boeing.

Merit vs. Diversity: The Debate Surrounding MEI and DEI Hiring Principles

The contemporary debate about hiring principles has taken an intriguing turn with the introduction of MEI (Merit, Excellence, and Intelligence), a new approach spearheaded by Alexandr Wang, CEO of Scale AI. MEI emphasizes hiring the best candidates based on merit, prioritizing excellence and intelligence without regard for demographic characteristics like race or gender.

Per the Adelaide Taylor "Merit vs. Diversity: The Debate Surrounding MEI and DEI Hiring Principles" B2B Daily June 2024 article:

Wang posits that a merit-based approach will naturally yield diverse backgrounds and ideas, underscoring the importance of treating individuals without stereotypes or tokenism. This principle has gained support among technological and business leaders, sparking a discussion about the implications for existing diversity, equity, and inclusion (DEI) strategies.

Support for MEI: The Case for a Merit-Based Approach

Prominent industry figures such as Elon Musk, Tobi Lutke, and Brian Armstrong have publicly endorsed the MEI principle, arguing that it fosters an unbiased, excellence-driven workforce. These supporters believe that hiring based solely on merit does not inherently conflict with achieving diversity.

According to them, the focus on excellence will naturally draw individuals from a wide array of backgrounds, thereby ensuring diversity without the need for explicitly designed DEI policies. The supporters of MEI assert that this approach can optimize a company's human resources by ensuring the best talents are recruited, leading to superior performance and innovation.

Elon Musk, for instance, has argued that hiring based solely on merit encourages a culture of high performance where employees are selected based on their abilities and potential rather than their demographic characteristics. This, he contends, can lead to a more innovative and productive workforce.

Tobi Lutke adds that in a truly meritocratic system, diversity is an organic byproduct, given that excellence is not confined to any single group. Consequently, proponents of MEI advocate for a focus on individual skills and achievements as a pathway to creating a diverse yet high-performing workforce.

Criticisms of MEI: Overlooking Systemic Biases

However, the MEI principle has faced significant criticism from DEI experts who argue that it overlooks the systemic biases and barriers that disproportionately affect underrepresented groups. Critics like Lisa Simon and Emily Witko argue that removing DEI policies risks regressing to homogeneous hiring patterns, where individuals tend to select candidates who resemble themselves. They emphasize that perceived merit often reflects the criteria defined by the current status quo, which can perpetuate existing inequalities rather than address them.

Lisa Simon points out that meritocratic systems, in their purest forms, assume a level playing field that does not exist in reality. She suggests that without policies that intentionally address historical and systemic inequities, organizations may inadvertently reinforce the advantages enjoyed by already privileged groups.

Emily Witko adds that DEI principles are designed to counteract these biases by creating opportunities for underrepresented groups and fostering a more inclusive environment that benefits everyone. Critics argue that a sole focus on merit can obscure the nuanced and multifaceted challenges of building genuinely inclusive workplaces.

Balancing Excellence with Inclusivity

The current discourse on hiring practices has taken a fascinating shift with the advent of MEI (Merit, Excellence, and Intelligence), a novel approach advocated by Alexandr Wang, CEO of Scale AI. MEI focuses on selecting top candidates based on their merit, placing a strong emphasis on excellence and intelligence without considering demographic factors such as race or gender.

Wang argues that a merit-based system will inherently result in a diverse pool of backgrounds and ideas, stressing the need to treat individuals free from stereotypes and tokenism.

This approach has garnered support among leaders in technology and business, igniting a debate on its implications for existing diversity, equity, and inclusion (DEI) strategies. Supporters believe that MEI could streamline hiring by focusing purely on individual capabilities, while critics worry that it might undermine the progress made in DEI initiatives.

The conversation continues to evolve, raising essential questions about how best to balance merit with the need for a diverse and inclusive workforce.

DEI or MEI: Which Builds Better Teams?

From Kevin Anderson, President of Power House Resources and his article titled "DEI or MEI: Which Builds Better Teams?" in *Energy Central* in July 2024:

As we navigate the complex landscape of workforce diversity and excellence, the debate between Diversity, Equity, and Inclusion (DEI) and Merit, Excellence, and Intelligence (MEI) continues to intrigue and challenge us. At Power House Resources, we strive to foster an environment where all individuals are valued for their contributions and talents, regardless of background or identity. The perspectives of DEI proponents, focusing on rectifying historical inequities, and MEI advocates, emphasizing individual merit and achievement, each bring valuable insights to the table.

As we explore these nuanced approaches, it becomes evident that both DEI and MEI aim to enhance workplace dynamics and foster a culture of inclusivity and excellence. This article delves into the strengths and considerations of each approach, inviting thoughtful reflection on how we can best achieve our shared goal of creating a fair and thriving workplace environment.

The Intersection of DEI and MEI: A Symphony of Approaches

The debate between Diversity, Equity, and Inclusion (DEI) and Merit, Excellence, and Intelligence (MEI) is akin to orchestrating a symphony. Just as each section of an orchestra plays a crucial role in creating a harmonious performance, DEI and MEI approaches bring distinct yet complementary perspectives to the workplace diversity debate.

MEI: Emphasizing Individual Excellence

Wang, CEO of Scale AI, champions MEI, advocating for hiring based solely on merit rather than demographic characteristics. Wang asserts that a merit-based system naturally fosters diversity, as excellence knows no demographic boundaries. "Scale is a meritocracy, and we must always remain one," Wang wrote. He emphasizes that talent should be the sole criterion, ensuring a variety of backgrounds, perspectives, and ideas contribute to organizational success.

Musk echoes this sentiment, critiquing DEI initiatives as potentially discriminatory. Musk argues that while aiming for equality, such initiatives can inadvertently prioritize traits over individual merit, thus perpetuating biases. "The point was to end discrimination, not replace it with different discrimination," Musk stated.

DEI: Addressing Historical Imbalances

Conversely, DEI proponents argue that such initiatives are crucial to rectifying historical and systemic inequities. They emphasize active efforts to ensure equal opportunities for all individuals, particularly those from marginalized groups. This perspective underscores the importance of representation and inclusivity in fostering a fair and just workplace.

A Symphony of Approaches

Imagine a symphony orchestra preparing for a performance. Each section—woodwinds, brass, strings, and percussion—represents a different aspect of the workplace diversity debate. The woodwinds symbolize DEI efforts, where each instrument contributes a unique voice to create harmony and balance. On the other hand, the brass section embodies MEI, with individual instruments showcasing their skill and excellence, blending together to create a powerful, cohesive sound.

Just as in an orchestra, where each section plays a crucial role in creating a masterpiece, DEI and MEI approaches bring valuable perspectives to the workplace. DEI strives to ensure all instruments have an equal opportunity to contribute, addressing historical inequities and promoting inclusivity. Meanwhile, MEI emphasizes the importance of individual talent and achievement, ensuring that each musician—regardless of background—has the chance to shine based on their merit.

Finding Common Ground

The challenge lies in harmonizing these approaches. Both DEI and MEI aim to create a competent and diverse talent pool. True diversity emerges when a variety of ideas and backgrounds are valued, selecting the most capable individuals without bias. A fair hiring process should neither advantage nor disadvantage any group but should ensure that all individuals are judged by their character, talent, and work ethic.

Raising Questions for HR Leaders

As HR leaders navigate these complex issues, several questions arise:

- How do you balance the principles of DEI and MEI in your organization's hiring practices?

- Have you encountered challenges or successes in integrating both approaches?

- Do you believe that focusing solely on merit naturally leads to diversity?

- How do you address potential biases within DEI and MEI frameworks?

- What strategies have proven effective in promoting an inclusive and excellent workforce?

Conclusion

In conclusion, while DEI and MEI may initially seem discordant, they both aim to create a workplace that is competent and diverse. The goal is to blend these principles to ensure fairness and excellence without compromising on either front. The ultimate objective is to recognize and value individuals for their merit, ensuring that everyone has an equal opportunity to contribute and succeed.

Moving from DEI to MEI: An Alternative Approach for Enhancing Workforce Performance

From the Dr. Vic Porak de Varna "Moving from DEI to MEI: An Alternative Approach for Enhancing Workforce Performance" LinkedIn post in October 2024: After reaching a peak, DEI is coming under increasing scrutiny by employers, courts, and legislatures. The reason is simple: DEI is unfair and doesn't work. There is a better alternative: Hiring based on "merit, excellence, and intelligence" or MEI.

DEI becomes divisive

Since reaching a high-water mark a few years ago, "diversity, equity, and inclusion" (DEI) initiatives are being rolled back across America. Critics like Elon Musk and investor Bill Ackman have called DEI efforts inherently unfair, illegal, and discriminatory. Companies like Tesla, Google, and Meta, and many others, have either eliminated or drastically scaled back their DEI programs.

The legal landscape is changing, too. Last year, the U.S. Supreme Court barred colleges and universities from using race as a factor in admissions. In a concurring opinion, Justice Gorsuch wrote that the same result should apply to private employers, and that race should not be a factor in hiring decisions. Meanwhile Florida and Texas have banned DEI in their colleges and universities.

The reason for the backlash is simple: DEI doesn't work. In fact, it runs against the mandate to hire regardless of race, ethnicity, gender, class, or sexual orientation. Moreover, studies show that DEI has negative consequences, including lower quality, lower productivity, and less innovation. It can also lead to lower product safety, as has happened at Boeing.

Instead of continuing a failing policy, leaders should look for ways to ensure they hire the best, brightest, and most qualified, regardless of background. This article will discuss an alternative to DEI and how leaders can make sure they are making the best hiring decisions now and in the future.

The MEI alternative

There is a better way. It has been called "Merit, Excellence, and Intelligence" (MEI). According to Scale AI Chief Executive Alexandr Wang, MEI calls for hiring the best candidates for open roles, regardless of background. Just as supporting DEI doesn't make a person tolerant of differences, supporting MEI doesn't make a person racist, sexist, or intolerant of differences.

As Wang says, "A hiring process based on merit will naturally yield a variety of backgrounds, perspectives, and ideas." He cautions, "We will not pick winners and losers based on someone being the 'right' or 'wrong' gender, race, and so on." As Elon Musk puts it, "The point was to end discrimination, not replace it with different discrimination." Even proponents of DEI concede that a large proportion of diversity interventions don't generate measurable positive results. Moreover, DEI "has been found to backfire on marginalized groups' feelings of belonging and weaken support for diversity programs when organizational performance drops," according to the *Harvard Business Review*.

In the MEI approach, hiring decisions are based strictly on merit. Diversity, whether of race, gender, or worldview, emerges naturally as the best candidates rise to the top. In other words, diversity isn't a goal to be chased by picking winners and losers in advance. It is simply the result of picking the best people for each role.

What's in a name? "Diversity" by other means

There's another problem with DEI: Organizations cannot mandate diversity through the hiring process. Unless they pick the best fit candidates, those candidates will leave, whether voluntarily because of poor fit, or involuntarily because of poor performance. You can't hold water in a colander.

The first line of defense against poor hiring decisions is to involve more people in the process to eliminate unconscious bias. We all enjoy being around people who share our interests, have similar experiences, and come from similar backgrounds. But that kind of bias can lead to problematic hiring decisions—and "problem" employees. MEI proponents report that group hiring decisions can lead to naturally diverse and successful workforces.

Once people are in place, the challenge is to keep them there. Excess turnover has a high cost and organizations have a vested interest in having their employees succeed. That's an area where DEI falls flat. We know what "diversity" means, but what qualifies as "equity" or "inclusion?"

"Equity" and "Inclusion"

Let's look at inclusion first. In a perfectly inclusive organization, nothing interferes with an employee's ability to perform at his or her peak. Things that can interfere with peak performance include not treating people with respect, making unreasonable workload demands, and not recognizing exceptional performance. To keep good people, organizations need to treat them fairly. It's as simple as that.

Now let's look at equity. That really means treating everyone the same way, without regard to background, race, gender, and so forth. That means paying equal salaries for equal roles and giving equal opportunities for training and advancement. When people see that organizations don't play favorites, they're more likely to stay.

The result of treating people fairly and equally is that more will stay, regardless of their backgrounds. With objective standards and a fair starting point, organizations can keep and retain a high performing workforce.

The time for DEI has passed. It's divisive, ineffective, and is receiving critical scrutiny from employers, courts, and legislatures. By contrast, MEI is inherently fair and doesn't pick winners and losers in advance. The time for MEI is now.

Why MEI Is Superior To DEI A Case For Merit, Excellence And Intelligence

In today's evolving discourse on workplace and societal values, the acronyms MEI (Merit, Excellence, and Intelligence) and DEI (Diversity, Equity, and Inclusion) often come into play per the Dr. Ken Keis "Why MEI Is Superior To DEI A Case For Merit, Excellence And Intelligence" Brainz Magazine article in September 2024:

While DEI has gained considerable traction in recent years, it's crucial to examine why MEI stands out as a far superior model, and why DEI, despite its good intentions, leads to destructive outcomes.

"Overhead view of two rowers in a rowing boat, with one wearing a sleeveless shirt and the other in a short-sleeved shirt, both holding oars in sync.

Now before individuals get defensive about this article, we are as a small company who has—had nine different cultures or backgrounds represented at the same time on our team. We do not endorse prejudice in anyway. I also sit on a global HR advisor group to assist HR leaders with the trends and impact that their policies are having on their organizations and cultures.

The challenge for many HR Leaders is they have lost sight of their primary responsibilities, which is to create a safe supportive environment, implementing systems which helps the organization succeed, and rewards individuals based on character and outcomes. Many have advocated these responsibilities to focus solely on DEI.

The Strengths of MEI

Merit

At the heart of MEI is merit—a principle that champions individuals based on their abilities, skills, and achievements. Meritocracy ensures that the most competent and qualified people rise to the top, driving excellence and innovation. It creates a clear, objective measure of success, where effort and talent are rewarded.

Excellence

Excellence pushes the boundaries of what's possible. It's about striving for the highest standards in every endeavor. Emphasizing excellence means fostering a culture of continuous improvement, where individuals and organizations are motivated to surpass previous achievements and deliver outstanding results.

Intelligence

Intelligence, in this context, refers to the capacity for critical thinking, problem-solving, and strategic decision-making. When intelligence is prioritized, decisions are based on sound reasoning and evidence, leading to better outcomes and more effective solutions.

MEI creates a robust framework that values hard work, skill, and intellectual capability. It encourages a culture where success is earned through merit, and standards are continually raised. This approach not only drives individual growth but also propels organizations and societies towards meaningful progress. In fact, MEI promote equality based on actual performance not some DEI mandate.

The Challenges of DEI

Diversity

On the surface, diversity seems like a noble goal—embracing a wide range of backgrounds, experiences, and perspectives. However, in practice, it leads to superficial changes rather than genuine improvement. When diversity initiatives prioritize representation over capability, they risk creating environments where positions are filled based on demographic factors rather than qualifications. This approach undermines the value of merit and excellence.

Equity

Equity aims to level the playing field by addressing perceived imbalances. While the intention is to rectify apparent injustices, the implementation can be problematic. By focusing on equal outcomes rather than equal opportunities, equity initiatives create new forms of bias. Instead of rewarding individual merit, they enforce policies that prioritize group characteristics over personal achievement, stifling talent and innovation.

Inclusion

Inclusion is about ensuring everyone feels valued and has a seat at the table. However, the push for inclusion can leads to tokenism or the dilution of standards. When organizations focus excessively on making everyone feel included, they inadvertently compromise on the quality of contributions. Inclusion efforts that prioritize comfort over challenge hinder critical discourse and diminish the drive for excellence.

The destructive impact of DEI

While DEI is often lauded for its commitment to fairness and representation, its application can lead to unintended negative consequences:

1. Dilution of standards

Prioritizing demographic characteristics over actual competence can dilute standards and undermine the quality of work. When the focus shifts from merit to mere representation, the overall effectiveness and excellence of teams and organizations suffer.

2. Promotion of mediocrity

 DEI initiatives that emphasize equity and inclusion without a strong merit-based foundation risk promoting mediocrity. By prioritizing equal outcomes over individual capability, organizations may end up rewarding less qualified individuals, which hinder progress and innovation.

3. Erosion of meritocracy

DEI's emphasis on demographic factors can erode the principles of meritocracy. When decisions are influenced more by identity politics than by performance and ability, it leads to resentment, division, and a lack of motivation among those who feel their efforts are overshadowed by less relevant factors.

4. Increased division

Paradoxically, DEI efforts actually exacerbate divisions rather than healing them. When policies are seen as favoring certain groups over others, it creates a sense of unfairness and division among employees or members of society. The focus on identity overshadows the need for unity and collective progress.

Example

I was personally contracted to conduct consulting, training and coaching for an international organization in a foreign country. When on site my internal company contact showed me someone in their office playing video games on their computer. This was a supervisory role and apparently all he did was play video games all day-everyday! He did not have the skills or intelligence for the position, nor the desire to work or fulfill the responsibilities of this role. However, because of DEI mandates in this organization, there was nothing that could be done. "He was part of the quota that was required."

What do you think this did to the entire culture of the company? Do you know who was leaving the organization "A" players—meaning individuals who could easily get employment elsewhere based on MEI. This left the organization with the lowest performing and least capable individuals.

As an expert in human performance and potential, there is and will be a long-term negative impact mentally and emotionally on the DEI hire! With video games filling his time—this is a person who has no purpose, drive, passion and little life fulfillment. As a result, he will have a strong propensity for depression and mental health issues. What a waste of a human life and his potential to contribute to society and make a difference.

Why MEI provides a better alternative

MEI's emphasis on merit, excellence, and intelligence fosters a culture where everyone is judged by their abilities and achievements. It creates an environment where hard work and talent are recognized and rewarded, leading to higher standards and better outcomes. Unlike DEI, which promotes mediocrity and division, MEI encourages a focus on genuine skill and capability.

In a world where success and progress are driven by the best and brightest, MEI stands out as a superior model. It ensures that individuals and organizations are motivated to excel based on their merits, pushing for continuous improvement and innovation. By valuing intelligence and excellence, MEI paves the way for true advancement and success, without the pitfalls associated with DEI.

While DEI initiatives have been introduced with the intention of creating fairer and more inclusive environments, they usually fall short of their goals and have a detrimental effect on performance and morale. MEI, on the other hand, offers a superior approach by focusing on merit, excellence, and intelligence, ensuring that individuals are recognized for their true capabilities and contributions. By embracing MEI, we can build a culture that truly rewards achievement and drives meaningful purpose and progress both individually and organizationally.

8 – Defeating Leftist DEI Madness by Cancelling the Cancellers

Credit: The Tack Online.

From the Katrina Gulliver "Cancelling the Cancellers" *City Journal* October 2023 article covering the new Foundation for Individual Rights and Expression (FIRE) book, *The Canceling of the American Mind: Cancel Culture Undermines Trust and Threatens Us All—But There Is a Solution*, by Greg Lukianoff and Rikki Schlott where Lukianoff considers how to upend the culture of fear on university campuses and beyond:

Greg Lukianoff, free-speech attorney, is back with a new book on the state of cancel culture. Lukianoff's previous book, *The Coddling of the American Mind* (co-written with Jonathan Haidt), addressed young people's emotional fragility and inability to handle conflict. In this new, similarly titled work, *The Canceling of the American Mind*, Lukianoff and coauthor Schlott turn their focus to the phenomenon of "cancellation": its origins, its corrosive effects, and how to push back against it.

Lukianoff and Schlott begin with a survey of cancel culture. They trace its origins to the anti-bullying movement, which told children to respond to bullying by telling an adult or a teacher about the mean kids. Proponents inculcated this approach among a whole generation. Those children have since grown up, and now, in the workplace, continue to "tell an adult" (in this case, their boss or HR) when conflicts arise.

Cancelling the Cancellers

Anyone born before 1985 likely grew up with a dim view of tattle-tales. (How many books and movies involve kids getting their own revenge on bullies by learning to fight back, and not involving any of the adults?)

The baby boomers saw the authorities as oppressive or irrelevant, to be ignored or rebelled against. Zoomers, by contrast, use the authorities as a dispute-resolution mechanism. In 1965, young people were sticking it to "the man"; in 2023, they demand that the man fire someone who uses a word they don't like on Facebook.

"The rise of Cancel Culture was not gradual," Lukianoff and Schlott observe. "On campuses across the country, it struck like lightning. Although students had long been generally supportive of free speech, a new generation of anti–free speech activists sprang up in the mid-2010s. Suddenly they were demanding speech codes, trigger warnings, and the policing of microaggressions."

The fuel of cancel culture is, of course, the power it gives to the cancellers. Teachers and professors can be canceled on the say-so of a motivated student. One shaky phone-camera video of a street argument can induce a life-changing hurricane of criticism that can escalate in some cases to ending a person's career.

We might be able to appreciate the thrill of turning the tables in a situation one finds unfair. And having complete strangers willing to jump in on your side? Power like that must be intoxicating. But that is an instinct we need to guard against, not just among the outrage-starters but also among those willing to join in, amplify, and validate the outrage.

The cancel crisis is not confined to America. "Although this book is focused on the United States," the authors write, "we will occasionally mention the insanity that has gone on in the United Kingdom, where hate speech laws can be deployed in service of Cancel Culture. In 2016 alone, more than 3,000 people were detained and questioned by police for non-crime 'hate incidents' related to what they had said on-line." This should terrify anyone who believes in free speech.

Cancel culture also can undermine public faith in institutions.

Many institutions, responding to cancellers' pressure, have nailed their colors to one political mast and declared the other side the enemy. The authors highlight the pandemic as an example, when the public broadly got the message "that our institutions cannot be trusted to produce an accurate, unbiased body of shared facts."

Lukianoff and Schlott propose rolling back the cancel-culture tide with both attitudinal and organizational changes. They suggest banning political litmus tests at American universities, including "mandatory DEI statements and other attempts to select students or professors who hold a 'preferred' political viewpoint," and "any conservative equivalent" to such statements.

The authors also point out that, far from being a left-only tactic, cancel campaigns in education have been launched from the right, too. The administrations of most colleges and universities lean left, of course, yet cancel campaigns from the right are sometimes successful, and even those that aren't can lead to people being threatened and harassed.

On the structural side, the authors propose allowing students to test out of college altogether and move straight to graduate school. They also advise alumni to look at their alma mater's record on free speech and adjust their donations accordingly. Such changes may help to stem the cancelation avalanche. But economics is a factor, too: academia has too few jobs for too many candidates, thus making cancel campaigns driven by professional rivalry more likely.

By contrast, job-rich fields tend to see fewer cancellation attempts; accountants and oil rig engineers don't face social media pile-ons the way academics do. This reality may be harder to address.

Canceling is in some sections a rehash of *Coddling*; readers familiar with Lukianoff's work will likely be able to hum its main melody if not sing the chorus. The book's argument is sensible, and the authors are optimistic that change is possible. The greatest obstacle to ending cancel culture, however, lies in converting those who deny it exists or who believe its victims had it coming. The people who most need to read this book won't.

Speaking Up: A New Bill Offers Hope of Protecting Free-Speech Rights at American Universities

In the summer of 2021, North Carolina congressman Greg Murphy introduced the Campus Free Speech Restoration Act, designed to enhance free expression in American universities. Murphy's bill defines "expressive activities" to include peaceful assembly, speaking, and listening and protects them from "improperly restrictive" institutional incursions, such as speech codes, bias response teams, and "free speech zones."

That legislation of this kind might be necessary is a sad commentary on academia. But as observers of American higher education know, college is now a place where free inquiry, free speech, and intellectual growth are imperiled. Surveys show that many professors and students now self-censor for political reasons. A punitive progressivism has become dogma, and vague harassment policies, zealous students, and ideological administrators chill dissent. Laws such as Murphy's can help, but it's vital to get the details right.

Public universities, legally subject to the First Amendment, get away with unconstitutional practices when authorities fail to respect and enforce the law. This is because no constitutional provision is self-enforcing. To give it effect, an injured party must sue a school. But after filing suit, that party often endures years of "lawfare"—stonewalling, appeals, trials, re-trials, and remands—that public universities, with taxpayer funds and lawyers at their disposal, greet with a yawn. All too often, individual lawsuits against universities are simply pebbles thrown against the citadel.

Murphy's bill addresses this problem with two innovations. First, it authorizes the Department of Education to condition Title IV federal funding on First Amendment compliance at public schools. While the bill does not specify how this would be implemented, it could easily appear alongside longstanding requirements in each school's Program Participation Agreement, which requires that institutions refrain from discriminating based on race and sex. The condition could also be the subject of an independent, annual certificate of compliance filed separately by the school with the Department of Education. The certification would force schools to document their efforts to protect free expression and to record where and when it was threatened—whether in "shout-downs," intimidation of speakers resulting in rescinded invitations or canceled lectures—and to list measures taken to prevent such events from recurring.

Second, the bill creates a new position in the Education Department to oversee the status of free speech on campus and to enforce the First Amendment there, independent of time-consuming and expensive litigation. This official would investigate credible complaints of First Amendment threats and would be authorized to impose penalties in the event of noncompliance.

(The bill also conditions Title IV funding for private universities on disclosure and enforcement of free-speech policies. This imposition is less demanding since private schools are not bound by the First Amendment.)

While the bill is a good start, practical questions remain.

Since the Department of Education's finding of noncompliance would remain reviewable by a court, does the bill's new federal review simply impose an extra bureaucratic layer on complainants? Won't this new Education Department official inevitably follow the policies of the administration in power? And, given that schools often cave soon after a complaint is filed by withdrawing contested policies—only to reintroduce the policies at a later date— how will the law prevent backsliding?

Modifications to the bill could account for some of these concerns. The legislation could further empower the Education Department position to conduct random audits on campuses to ensure that a school's culture, policies, and enforcement practices are First Amendment–friendly. The new office need not wait passively to receive complaints, but instead, like health and safety agencies, should proactively inspect premises to prevent injury.

The bill could also authorize the official to enjoin the problematic policy or action when a complaint makes a reasonable case of a likely violation. The burden of proof at this early stage would be intentionally low—in favor of the complaint and of free expression. This would help level the "lawfare" playing field, signal the importance of the First Amendment in the academic setting, and recognize the reality that institutions of higher learning no longer deserve the benefit of the doubt on speech issues.

Finally, the bill should require the Department of Education to notify a school's regents or trustees of any complaint, investigation, or injunction, as well as the associated costs. The board can then communicate with the general assembly to deduct such costs from the school's annual appropriations, which would, of course, be refunded or re-appropriated should a final judgment exonerate the school.

Taken together, these provisions would ensure that the institution bears the cost of likely constitutional violations—not the individual and not the taxpayers. More could be said about required elements for injunctive relief and about finding the right person to fill this new position. But with time and some tinkering, Murphy's legislation could be an important step toward rescuing American higher education.

Like the other proposed solutions in this section that address the freedom of speech and expression suppression taking place throughout America's educational institutions, the Free Speech Alumni Ambassador (FSAA) Program can be the catalyst to help make them happen.

How to Defeat Left-Wing Racialism

From the joint team of Wade Miller, Dan Morenoff, Ilya Shapiro, David E. Bernstein, James Sherk, Judge Glock, Christopher F. Rufo comes the article "How to Defeat Left-Wing Racialism" in the Summer 2023 *City Journal* reporting on a symposium on restoring the principle of color blindness brought together seven sapient scholars, researchers, and journalists together to collaborate on this insightful article and its action plan.

The summer of 2020 was a watershed in American life. After George Floyd's death in police custody and the ensuing season of rioting, major institutions—from federal agencies to Fortune 100 companies—hastily pledged themselves to the narrative of critical race theory, which holds that America is a fundamentally racist nation and that public and private entities should practice "antiracist discrimination" to equalize group outcomes—a state of affairs that its advocates call "racial equity."

This ideology stands in direct opposition to the principles of the Constitution, which provides for color-blind equality under law. Yet many American institutions quickly adopted "diversity, equity, and inclusion" policies, such as discriminatory hiring practices and racially segregated employee groups, that are, correctly interpreted, illegal.

We have convened a symposium with six of the nation's leading domestic-policy experts and asked them to consider how future policymakers might restore the principle of color-blind equality in government. Their recommendations are not comprehensive. But they would start the process—already begun, perhaps, by the Supreme Court's ruling that race-based college admissions policies are unconstitutional—of restraining the forces of left-wing racialism and moving the country back toward a regime of individual merit and fair treatment under law.

Defund the Left

The fight against a woke and weaponized federal government has begun, though it remains in its early stages. Wokeness in the federal government is best understood as a method of decision-making by activist bureaucrats. They determine how taxpayer money gets spent, who benefits, who loses, and which social-justice cause gets prioritized in government programming. Dismantling their taxpayer-funded supply lines is a critical element in defeating their efforts.

How to do this? For starters, Congress should continue to reduce nondefense discretionary spending and budget authority to pre-Covid levels—not just to curb inflation and bend the curve of the national debt but to reduce the power of the federal agencies and departments that have pursued agendas that stoke racial division.

A key component in the next budget fight should be ending competitive grant programs, most of which fund far-left organizations that use public money to advance their causes. The Appropriations Committee should turn off the competitive grant spigot altogether, or, at a minimum, include legislative and limitation riders that prohibit such funding from promoting divisive racialist theories.

The Rules Committee, meantime, should adopt new standards as part of the budget and appropriations process to forbid floor amendments that fund programs, agencies, or nongovernmental entities practicing diversity, equity, and inclusion (DEI). In tandem, lawmakers should consider more aggressive use of the Holman Rule, which lets House members cut specific programs and fire specific employees. This tool can be deployed to defund DEI departments and hold activist bureaucrats accountable to Congress.

Lastly, every House committee chairman should hold hearings that scrutinize the woke bureaucracies under their respective purviews. These congressional efforts will help build a public case against DEI and lay the groundwork for executive actions in a new administration.

Mobilize the Department of Justice Against Racialist Discrimination

An equality-friendly administration will need to prioritize its options for reversing the spread of racialist ideology across American institutions. Two initiatives should head the list.

First, the Department of Justice (DOJ) and other enforcement agencies should once again take seriously their obligation to ensure that our public and private institutions comply with Title VI of the Civil Rights Act and cease racial discrimination—including so-called antiracist discrimination based on critical race theory, which rewards or punishes individuals according to their racial identity.

To this end, the next administration should swiftly instruct all agencies to initiate investigations nationwide against entities that discriminate based on race and pursue cutting off federal funding for institutions that refuse to comply. Targets should include schools and universities and local and state governments. The Equal Employment Opportunity Commission should investigate corporations. The DOJ and EEOC should stand ready to follow through with litigation.

In education, this would mean probing many of the large school systems, including those in San Francisco, Boston, New York, and Northern Virginia, that have altered admissions policies to reduce the number of Asian Americans in magnet schools. Additionally, it would mean investigating many universities for discriminatory admissions policies (which the Supreme Court recently deemed unconstitutional) and racially segregated scholarships. University of Michigan professor emeritus Mark Perry has identified hundreds of these programs; all should be shut down.

Second, in partnership with the Securities and Exchange Commission and the Federal Trade Commission, the DOJ should investigate the three largest passive-investment firms—BlackRock, Vanguard, and State Street—for antitrust violations. These firms have aggressively promoted environmental, social, and governance (ESG) initiatives, which often encourage discriminatory racial quotas or segregated employee groups.

Federal investigators should look for collusion in these firms' mutual participation in ESG activist initiatives and examine their lockstep adoption and advancement of parallel ESG goals.

As part of this investigation, the agencies should question the Clayton Antitrust Act's impact on these giant firms' joint control over vast swaths of the economy. Two of the "Big Three" are publicly traded—and the two largest owners of each are the other two, leaving the firms in apparent control of each other. The Big Three, jointly, are the largest shareholders in almost the entire S&P 500 stock-market index. They appear to hold joint control of 14 of America's 15 largest banks. If they are in violation of the Clayton Act, the government could force them to divest themselves from one another and bar them from colluding to promote adoption of discriminatory ESG policies. Good antitrust policy would be good civil rights policy.

These two initiatives would represent a starting point for reestablishing the government's commitment to equality for all.

Force Open Debate on Campus

Higher education is in crisis. Students and faculty are uncomfortable speaking their minds, lest they find themselves canceled; tuition costs are skyrocketing, far in excess of inflation; taxpayers are asking why they're paying for radical indoctrination.

This crisis is the result of an exploding university bureaucracy that subverts faculty governance in favor of an illiberal identitarianism. What began as administrative bloat has become a full-blown commissariat that stifles intellectual diversity, undermines equal opportunity, and excludes dissenting voices. The average four-year university now has more DEI officials than history professors. DEI offices have broadened the meaning of terms like "harassment" and "discrimination" not to promote a welcoming campus environment but to enforce progressive ideology.

How do we fix this mess? Appeals for internal reform aren't enough. The problem necessitates external controls from federal agencies, civil rights regulators, and congressional oversight, tied to federal funding.

Fortunately, Congress has already given the Department of Education (DOE) some tools to address these issues. The next administration should instruct the department to compel institutions to certify their compliance with federal requirements on the protection of student speech and association rights and with Supreme Court rulings that outlaw loyalty oaths.

Conservatives Mandates

Just as all recipients of federal higher-education funds must certify compliance on everything from accounting standards to antidiscrimination practices, conservatives can mandate that they discontinue programs that undermine free speech and due process, as well as those that constitute compelled speech in the form of diversity statements.

Next, the Office of Civil Rights (OCR) should investigate any institution that admits to engaging in "systemic" or "structural" racism, as was claimed in so many self-flagellating statements three summers ago. In addition, to ensure that colleges and universities don't resist the Supreme Court's recent ruling that bans racial preferences in admissions, the OCR should require them to show that their admissions processes are indeed color-blind—whether by disclosing GPA and standardized test data, or by another method that prevents racial discrimination by proxy.

Finally, the DOE must overhaul accreditation metrics to focus on fraud prevention and academic rigor and must remove accreditation monopolies, such as the one that the American Bar Association enjoys over law schools, when institutions abandon (as the ABA has) their mission of neutral, merit-based judgment.

There's still a long way to go before higher education returns to its mission of seeking truth, but the next Department of Education has a vital role to play in advancing that process.

Roll Back Racial Classifications

In 1977, the federal government issued Statistical Directive No. 15, establishing America's official racial and ethnic classifications: black, white, Hispanic, Asian, and Native American. The purpose was to create uniform classifications, so that data for endeavors like civil rights enforcement and educational achievement could be shared and compared across government agencies. Nevertheless, the classifications quickly spread through American law and society and are now used for everything from college admissions to scientific research.

The problem: Directive 15 classifications are arbitrary and inconsistent, both in how they are defined and how they are enforced. The government developed its classifications through a combination of amateur sociology, interest-group lobbying, incompetence, inertia, and happenstance. The classifications never made much sense beyond the historical black–white divide. Now, given the country's dramatic demographic changes since 1977, they border on incoherence. It's time to reconsider them.

First, the next administration should review every instance in which the government uses, or requires private parties to use, racial classifications. These identity-group categories are inherently illiberal and divisive. Consistent with Supreme Court precedent, the government should get out of the racial-classification business entirely, unless a "compelling interest" exists for using such classifications.

Second, the administration should abolish the regulations that force biomedical researchers to classify their subjects and report data based on the Directive 15 classifications. These classifications have no plausible scientific justification; they absorb resources better spent on scientific advances; and they have stunted the development of therapies based on genetics.

Third, the next administration should reverse the Biden administration's plans to turn the Hispanic ethnic classification into a racial one and to add new Middle Eastern and North African (MENA) classifications. If implemented, both proposals would make our already-incoherent, arbitrary classification system even worse.

Fourth, to the extent that racial classifications do serve a compelling government interest, their use should be narrowly tailored to that purpose. One model to look at is the FBI's hate-crime statistics. The agency tabulates such crimes against 29 identifiable groups, among them Mormons and gender-nonconforming people.

Finally, to the extent that the Directive 15 classifications continue to be used, it makes sense, in many instances, to break up the broad, crude classifications into ethnic and national-origin subcategories. The "white" classification, for example, includes people with descent anywhere from Iceland to Yemen. "Asian" includes Bangladeshis and Filipinos. Limiting the data to the broad classifications, rather than digging deeper into their constituent parts, can obscure more than it illuminates.

Balance the Federal Workforce—Intellectually

Some argue that civil rights laws can protect Americans from woke discrimination. That will not happen without significantly more viewpoint diversity in the federal bureaucracy. The federal workforce leans well to the left. Democrats outnumber Republicans about two-to-one. Headquarters employees live in an even more liberal environment: in Washington, D.C., Joe Biden took 93 percent of the vote.

In theory, civil servants' political views should not matter. In practice, conservative presidents frequently face internal resistance from long-serving bureaucrats with different political beliefs.

This is especially true in civil rights agencies. They naturally appeal to progressive activists who, once hired, systematically hire like-minded colleagues. During President Obama's first term, one DOJ Civil Rights Division (CRD) section almost exclusively hired left-wing activists into career positions.

This imbalance makes evenhanded enforcement of civil rights protections challenging. The woke employees who dominate the bureaucracy have no interest in combating woke discrimination.

For example, a DOJ investigation found that Yale University was discriminating against Asian and Caucasian applicants. Trump administration officials wanted to sue, but CRD career staff refused to participate in the litigation. The DOJ could bring charges only by using political appointees and detailing staff from other divisions. Career staff then dropped the case when President Biden took office.

Agencies have few political appointees; they rely on career employees for routine enforcement. Progressive domination of the career bureaucracy makes systematically enforcing protections against woke discrimination impossible.

Increase Intellectual Diversity

The only solution is to increase intellectual diversity in the federal bureaucracy. Instead of focusing diversity initiatives on race or other protected characteristics, federal agencies should seek an intellectually balanced workforce. To achieve this, they should actively try to hire career employees whose worldviews differ from those of current staff.

In some departments, this might mean hiring more progressive employees. But in most, including the civil rights agencies, fostering intellectual diversity would mean recruiting and hiring more moderates and conservatives.

This can be done in several ways. The agencies could recruit new career staff from public-interest law firms like the Pacific Legal Foundation, Alliance Defending Freedom, and the Center for Individual Rights, or from red-state attorneys general offices. Similarly, they could proactively recruit graduates of conservative-leaning schools.

Federal agencies don't need a majority of their workforce to be conservative. They do need a critical mass of career employees who will enforce laws that activists on either side might oppose.

American society contains an enormous range of views. To a large extent, the career federal workforce—especially in civil rights agencies—does not. Until that changes, civil rights enforcement will not protect all Americans from discrimination.

End Minority Contracting

The practice of favoring minority-owned firms in government contracts, though it does not get the headlines of affirmative-action plans in schools or workplaces, may have an even bigger impact. (See "Welcome to the World of Minority Contracting," Spring 2023.)

Federal, state, and local governments use "set asides" and no-bid deals to ensure that anywhere from 5 percent to 30 percent of their contracts go to minority businesses. Since nearly one-tenth of the American economy runs through government contracts, the consequences of these programs are significant. However, instead of righting historical wrongs, minority contracting has produced corruption and fraud, worsened racial tensions, and cost taxpayers billions of dollars.

We have lots of evidence that these programs encourage fraud. A 2016 Department of Transportation presentation stated that more than one-third of its contracting-fraud cases involved minority contracting. Whether it's construction at Chicago O'Hare International Airport, snow-removal deals in Atlanta, or casino projects in New York, minority-owned front companies often take a small cut and pass the work on to a white contractor, making a mockery of attempts to help the truly disadvantaged.

The result is significantly higher costs for taxpayers. Economist Justin Marion examined contracts on California highway projects before and after state voters banned racial preferences. Costs on the California projects dropped 5.6 percent compared with federally funded projects in which racial preferences remained in place. Studies of minority contracting show little or no positive effects on minority entrepreneurship.

How are these programs justified? In two cases, the Supreme Court said that governments could use racial contracting preferences only to remedy actual government discrimination. Instead of restraining such efforts, however, these cases spawned an industry for bogus "disparity studies" that legitimate them.

The solution is simple: Congress should end minority-contracting programs and ban the consideration of race (or sex) in all business decisions. As government continues to grow, Americans of all races don't want to spare ever more funds for ever worse service. They don't want their infrastructure projects sabotaged by costly requirements about the race of their contractors. And they don't want the government to enrich a small group of politically connected businesses that somehow get to claim the mantle of discrimination.

9 – The Time is Now to Dismantle DEI Programs Throughout America

Credit: Photo illustration by Justin Morrison/Inside Higher Ed.

In June 2023, the Supreme Court effectively ended race-based affirmative action in higher education in the Students for Fair Admissions (SFFA) case. On the heels of that decision, newly empowered activists have brought a barrage of challenges.

What happens when the irresistible force meets the immovable object? Leaders committed to diversity, equity, and inclusion (DEI) are facing this paradox with fresh urgency these days as reported in the Kenji Yoshino and David Glasgow "DEI Is Under Attack. Here's How Companies Can Mitigate the Legal Risks" *Harvard Business Review* January 2024 article:

The irresistible force is represented by the mounting legal assault on DEI. In June 2023, the Supreme Court effectively ended race-based affirmative action in higher education in the Students for Fair Admissions (SFFA) case. On the heels of that decision, newly empowered activists have brought a barrage of challenges against workplace DEI efforts. Major companies are being slapped with formal complaints, litigation, and threatening letters.

DEI Is Under Attack. Here's How Companies Can Mitigate the Legal Risks

While the outcome of any particular effort is rife with uncertainties, the overall direction of the law under a 6–3 Supreme Court conservative supermajority is not one of them. As such, some wonder whether DEI work is coming to an end. As one left-leaning legal scholar asked rhetorically: "If your whole job description has been to press for diversity, especially racial diversity, what are you supposed to do when pursuing that objective has been rendered effectively illegal?"

Yet the force of the legal assault on DEI is hitting an immovable object. As Justice Sonia Sotomayor pointed out in her dissent in SFFA, "Diversity is now a fundamental American value, housed in our varied and multicultural community that only continues to grow."

Too many people in too many major institutions, including leaders of corporations, government, academia, and the military are committed to DEI for it to disappear. As one right-leaning journalist observed, it's foolish for activists to think they can "end DEI," as "that's not going to happen."

What, then, will occur when the force of the law collides with one of the deeply held beliefs of the twenty-first century? We predict that neither side will "win." Rather, as the law inevitably evolves in a more conservative direction, the new legal standards will be absorbed into the field of DEI, transforming it as an enterprise. While this shift will occur organically, smart organizations can avoid a lot of pain and expense by thinking about how to adapt in a more intentional way.

What Makes DEI Risky?

To recognize what shifts are necessary, we must start by assessing legal risk. A DEI program is most risky when it meets three criteria:

1. It confers a preference, meaning that some individuals are treated more favorably than others.

2. The preference is given to members of a legally protected group, such as groups defined by the categories protected in Title VII of the Civil Rights Act of 1964. These are race, color, religion, national origin, and sex (including sexual orientation and gender identity).

3. The preference relates to a palpable benefit, such as a job, a promotion, a pay raise, a work assignment, or access to training and development opportunities.

With these three criteria in mind, it is possible to identify risky DEI programs. They include:

- Hiring quotas ("Make sure at least 45% of our incoming associates are women")

- Tiebreaker decision-making ("If you're choosing between two similarly strong candidates and one is white and the other is a person of color, pick the person of color")

- Group-specific internships and fellowships ("Let's create an internship that limits eligibility to Black and Latino talent")

- Tying manager compensation to diversity goals ("You will get a bonus if you hire more women and people of color on your team")

All four of these programs confer a preference on members of protected groups with respect to palpable benefits. Of course, many defenders of such programs rightly point out that these initiatives do not actually involve a "preference," but rather simply compensate for biases that have systematically deprived certain groups of opportunities. Unfortunately, however, it is clear that the conservative supermajority on the Supreme Court does not agree with such a worldview.

These three risk criteria also point the way to how organizations can mitigate risk in their DEI programs: avoid preferences, avoid protected groups, or avoid palpable benefits.

Avoid Preferences: From Lifting to Leveling

Rather than giving "preference" to some groups, organizations can explore DEI actions that are identity-neutral but remove bias from the workplace. Examples include creating structured recruitment and promotion processes with clear, transparent, merit-based criteria; removing stereotypical language from employee evaluation processes; and reviewing employee benefits policies to ensure they are being applied equally. These approaches do not "lift" certain groups above others, but rather "level" the playing field for everybody.

Even under a worst-case scenario legal landscape, such leveling approaches will remain legal, because anti-discrimination law only applies when some people are treated differently from others.

Avoid Protected Groups: Up-switching, Down-switching, and Side-switching

The next option for reducing legal liability is to avoid protected characteristics such as race or sex. There are three ways of doing so.

The first is to shift from "cohorts to content," or what we call "up-shifting." Instead of limiting participation in DEI programs to members of particular cohorts, organizations can open participation to people of all demographic backgrounds who are committed to the content of the program. In a recent high-profile example, three major law firms were sued for diversity fellowship programs that limited eligibility to members of underrepresented groups. As soon as the firms changed the eligibility criteria to include anyone with a demonstrated commitment to diversity and inclusion, the lawsuits were dropped.

The second option is to shift from "cohorts to character" (down-shifting). This means considering a candidate's identity only where it speaks to their individual character. In the SFFA decision, the court pointedly noted that while universities could no longer give a bump to candidates based on their race, they could still consider "an applicant's discussion of how race affected his or her life, be it through discrimination, inspiration, or otherwise."

The same applies to employers. While employers cannot make, say, a promotion decision based on race, they could invite candidates for promotion to submit an essay describing how their race and other aspects of identity have affected their lives. The employer could then consider those individual experiences when deciding which candidates have displayed resilience, determination, or other important leadership qualities.

The final option for avoiding protected groups is to shift from "cohorts to cohorts" (side-switching). This means shifting from cohorts protected by laws such as Title VII to cohorts that are not protected in such ways. For example, an organization could adopt a program that advances socioeconomic diversity, given that socioeconomic status is not a protected attribute under federal anti-discrimination law. Provided the organization is not using the new cohort as a proxy for a protected one, this form of side-switching is legally sound.

Avoid Palpable Benefits: From Adverse to Ambient

Organizations also can reduce legal risk by avoiding palpable benefits. Under Title VII, plaintiffs need to have suffered an "adverse employment action" to bring a discrimination claim, meaning a concrete change in their terms or conditions of employment rather than a mere inconvenience or trivial slight. Similarly, under another federal law that is currently being used to challenge DEI programs—section 1981 of the Civil Rights Act of 1866 — claimants need to have experienced discrimination in the making or enforcement of a contract.

As such, one safe harbor for organizations is to create DEI programs that build a more diverse and inclusive workplace culture overall, but do not directly affect the benefits or employment opportunities of individual workers. For instance, organizations might:

- Conduct employee education or training on topics such as bias, allyship, or inclusive leadership

- Create a more physically inclusive office environment, for example through all-gender bathrooms, nursing rooms, or child-care facilities

- Conduct outreach to a broader range of colleges to attract a more diverse candidate pool

- Support community organizations focused on DEI issues, for example through pro bono work and philanthropy

This term, the Supreme Court will decide a case that could lower the standard for what counts as an "adverse employment action," making it easier to challenge some DEI programs. For now, however, organizations can mitigate risk by embracing a more "ambient" approach to their work.

Putting It All Together

These three shifts respond to the seemingly unanswerable question of what happens when the irresistible force meets the immovable object. The answer is that the object changes. The force is not resisted; it is absorbed. And the object is not moved; it is transformed.

It is true that the law will force the practice of DEI to change significantly. Yet so long as champions of DEI shift it in these strategic ways, DEI's core project of building a more just future will endure for decades to come.

Executive Order: Ending Radical and Wasteful Government DEI Programs and Preferencing

One of many executive orders that President Trump signed into action in January 2025 is the Executive Order: Ending Radical and Wasteful Government DEI Programs and Preferencing as follows:

By the authority vested in me as President by the Constitution and the laws of the United States of America, it is hereby ordered:

Section 1. Purpose and Policy. The Biden Administration forced illegal and immoral discrimination programs, going by the name "diversity, equity, and inclusion" (DEI), into virtually all aspects of the Federal Government, in areas ranging from airline safety to the military. This was a concerted effort stemming from President Biden's first day in office, when he issued Executive Order 13985, "Advancing Racial Equity and Support for Underserved Communities Through the Federal Government."

Pursuant to Executive Order 13985 and follow-on orders, nearly every Federal agency and entity submitted "Equity Action Plans" to detail the ways that they have furthered DEIs infiltration of the Federal Government. The public release of these plans demonstrated immense public waste and shameful discrimination. That ends today. Americans deserve a government committed to serving every person with equal dignity and respect, and to expending precious taxpayer resources only on making America great.

Sec. 2. Implementation. (a) The Director of the Office of Management and Budget (OMB), assisted by the Attorney General and the Director of the Office of Personnel Management (OPM), shall coordinate the termination of all discriminatory programs, including illegal DEI and "diversity, equity, inclusion, and accessibility" (DEIA) mandates, policies, programs, preferences, and activities in the Federal Government, under whatever name they appear. To carry out this directive, the Director of OPM, with the assistance of the Attorney General as requested, shall review and revise, as appropriate, all existing Federal employment practices, union contracts, and training policies or programs to comply with this order. Federal employment practices, including Federal employee performance reviews, shall reward individual initiative, skills, performance, and hard work and shall not under any circumstances consider DEI or DEIA factors, goals, policies, mandates, or requirements.

(b) Each agency, department, or commission head, in consultation with the Attorney General, the Director of OMB, and the Director of OPM, as appropriate, shall take the following actions within sixty days of this order:

(i)   terminate, to the maximum extent allowed by law, all DEI, DEIA, and "environmental justice" offices and positions (including but not limited to "Chief Diversity Officer" positions); all "equity action plans," "equity" actions, initiatives, or programs, "equity-related" grants or contracts; and all DEI or DEIA performance requirements for employees, contractors, or grantees.

(ii)   provide the Director of the OMB with a list of all:

(A) agency or department DEI, DEIA, or "environmental justice" positions, committees, programs, services, activities, budgets, and expenditures in existence on November 4, 2024, and an assessment of whether these positions, committees, programs, services, activities, budgets, and expenditures have been misleadingly relabeled in an attempt to preserve their pre-November 4, 2024 function;

(B) Federal contractors who have provided DEI training or DEI training materials to agency or department employees; and

(C) Federal grantees who received Federal funding to provide or advance DEI, DEIA, or "environmental justice" programs, services, or activities since January 20, 2021.

(iii) direct the deputy agency or department head to:

(A) assess the operational impact (e.g., the number of new DEI hires) and cost of the prior administration's DEI, DEIA, and "environmental justice" programs and policies; and

(B) recommend actions, such as Congressional notifications under 28 U.S.C. 530D, to align agency or department programs, activities, policies, regulations, guidance, employment practices, enforcement activities, contracts (including set-asides), grants, consent orders, and litigating positions with the policy of equal dignity and respect identified in section 1 of this order. The agency or department head and the Director of OMB shall jointly ensure that the deputy agency or department head has the authority and resources needed to carry out this directive.

(c) To inform and advise the President, so that he may formulate appropriate and effective civil-rights policies for the Executive Branch, the Assistant to the President for Domestic Policy shall convene a monthly meeting attended by the Director of OMB, the Director of OPM, and each deputy agency or department head to:

(i) hear reports on the prevalence and the economic and social costs of DEI, DEIA, and "environmental justice" in agency or department programs, activities, policies, regulations, guidance, employment practices, enforcement activities, contracts (including set-asides), grants, consent orders, and litigating positions;

(ii) discuss any barriers to measures to comply with this order; and

(iii) monitor and track agency and department progress and identify potential areas for additional Presidential or legislative action to advance the policy of equal dignity and respect.

Sec. 3. Severability. If any provision of this order, or the application of any provision to any person or circumstance, is held to be invalid, the remainder of this order and the application of its provisions to any other persons or circumstances shall not be affected.

Sec. 4. General Provisions. (a) Nothing in this order shall be construed to impair or otherwise affect:

(i) the authority granted by law to an executive department or agency, or the head thereof; or

(ii) the functions of the Director of the Office of Management and Budget relating to budgetary, administrative, or legislative proposals.

(b) This order shall be implemented consistent with applicable law and subject to the availability of appropriations.

(c) This order is not intended to, and does not, create any right or benefit, substantive or procedural, enforceable at law or in equity by any party against the United States, its departments, agencies, or entities, its officers, employees, or agents, or any other person.

THE WHITE HOUSE,

January 20, 2025.

Cloud and Schmitt Introduce Bill to Codify into Law Trump's Agenda Ending DEI in Federal Government

Congressman Michael Cloud (TX-27) and Senator Eric Schmitt (R-MO) have introduced in February 2025 the Dismantle DEI Act, a bill to codify into law President Trump's agenda dismantling so-called Diversity, Equity, and Inclusion (DEI) programs across the federal government. This legislation ensures that Trump's actions are permanently enshrined in law, preventing future administrations from reviving these divisive and wasteful policies.

When President Biden took office, he issued Executive Order 13985, embedding DEI into nearly every federal agency. These programs required agencies to prioritize racial, gender, and identity preferences over merit and performance. Biden further expanded this by creating "Chief Diversity Officers" and mandating "Equity Action Plans," diverting taxpayer dollars toward programs that undermined fairness and promoted division.

On day one of his Presidency, Donald Trump reversed these actions by issuing an executive order to rescind DEI mandates, eliminate related offices, and halt programs promoting these divisive policies. The Dismantle

DEI Act complements Trump's actions by permanently banning such programs and ensuring they cannot be brought back under new names or disguised titles.

The Dismantle DEI Act:

- Defines and prohibits DEI practices to prevent future administrations from reinstating similar Biden-era DEI policies.

- Ensures all DEI offices are terminated and prohibits agencies from renaming or repurposing them to continue the same functions under new titles.

- Bars federal funds from being used for DEI training, grants, or programs—including identity-based quotas and critical race theory.

- Grants individuals the legal right to challenge any of these violations in court.

The Dismantle DEI Act extends beyond federal agencies, impacting federal contractors, grant recipients, and accreditation bodies. It removes federal support for divisive DEI mandates that have proliferated in both government and private industry, ensuring taxpayer dollars are no longer used to perpetuate these policies.

The legislation comes as federal DEI programs have ballooned under President Biden's "whole-of-government" approach to racial equity. These initiatives include mandatory DEI training for nuclear engineers, military commanders, and IRS staff. For example, a Sandia National Laboratories training instructed engineers to confront "white male culture," which it defined as exhibiting traits like "a can-do attitude" and "hard work."

Christopher Rufo of the Manhattan Institute also obtained that the 2019 training session was led by the group "White Men As Full Diversity Partners," nuclear weapons engineers were instructed to craft brief messages directed at "white women" and "people of color" to convey what they had learned from the experience.

The Act would also save taxpayers billions by slashing wasteful spending. In 2023 alone, the Biden administration allocated over $16 million for DEI-related training and requested $83 million for similar initiatives at the State

Department. DEI policies in health and science funding, particularly through the National Institutes of Health, have diverted billions into programs that prioritize DEI.

FEMA's DEI Priority Highlight Need for Reform

During a November 2024 House Oversight Committee hearing, Rep. Cloud criticized FEMA's response to Hurricanes Milton and Helene, pointing to its 2022-2026 Strategic Plan, which lists "Instill Equity as a Foundation of Emergency Management" as its top priority. "Emergency management should be about saving lives and helping all Americans—not pushing divisive agendas," Cloud said at the time. FEMA's failures during these disasters exemplify how DEI policies have real-world implications for the well-being of American citizens.

Corporate America Retreats from DEI Mandates

The push to dismantle DEI is part of a broader trend. Over the past year, companies like Walmart, Ford, Meta, and Amazon have significantly scaled back their DEI programs, citing inefficiencies, public dissatisfaction, and divisive outcomes. If major corporations are retreating from DEI mandates, it's time for the federal government to follow suit.

The Dismantle DEI Act addresses one of the most pressing challenges of our time by confronting the pervasive influence of divisive DEI policies. It reflects the overwhelming desire of the American people to prioritize merit and hard work over immutable characteristics, ensuring their tax dollars support initiatives that unite rather than divide.

This legislation complements President Trump's Executive Order issued on January 20th, which set the stage for eliminating DEI mandates across the federal government. The Dismantle DEI Act takes those efforts a step further by codifying them into law, ensuring that these divisive and wasteful policies are permanently dismantled. Together, these actions reaffirm our commitment to merit, accountability, and the principle that every American deserves a government that serves with equal dignity and respect.

"DEI was never about fairness or opportunity—it was a Trojan horse for left-wing political social engineering that fosters division, not unity," said Congressman Cloud. "Hiring and promotion should be because of someone's merit, excellence, and hard work, regardless of race, religion, or creed. The Dismantle DEI Act is about restoring common sense, ensuring taxpayer dollars are used wisely, and refocusing the federal government on serving all Americans fairly.

I'm grateful to President Trump for reversing these harmful policies on Day 1 of his Administration. His leadership put an end to these divisive, un-American programs, and it's now Congress's job to follow through and codify the permanent elimination of DEI from our government."

"Diversity, Equity, and Inclusion (DEI) programs have plagued our federal government, academic institutions, and other aspects of our society, cheapening standards while disregarding merit," said Senator Schmitt. "Moreover, taxpayer dollars should not be wasted on this poisonous, divisive ideology. These programs have absolutely no business in our federal government, and I am proud to reintroduce this critical bill that will save taxpayer dollars and put a stop to the DEI madness."

"The DEI agenda has no place in our federal government. It is nothing more than a Trojan horse designed to push radical, divisive policies under the false pretense of inclusion," said Peter Holland, Foundation for Government Accountability. "I'm grateful to Rep. Cloud for taking bold action with the Dismantle DEI Act. Now, taxpayer-funded agencies and programs can refocus on merit and their core mission to address the real issues Americans care about instead of wasting time on a subversive, politically motivated DEI agenda."

"Americans have long known that DEI policies have nothing to do with preventing discrimination and everything to do with marshaling the power of the state and other institutions to discriminate against and punish the Left's perceived 'oppressor classes,'" said Ryan Walker, Heritage Action. "The Dismantle DEI Act safeguards equal protection under the law for all Americans regardless of race or sex, unlike our current system. Heritage Action encourages Congress to dismantle the illegal DEI regime entrenched in the federal government."

10 – Restoring MEI in Academia, Government & Corporate America

Credit: President Trump at his desk | President Donald J. Trump is s... | Flickr.

According to the Christopher F. Rufo "Giving DEI the Pink Slip" *City Journal* article in March 2024 major institutions have started rolling back their diversity bureaucracies:

Last year, conservatives began taking action against the "diversity, equity, and inclusion" bureaucracy. The Manhattan Institute released a model policy to abolish DEI, exposed abuses in public universities, and advised political leaders, most notably Florida governor Ron DeSantis, in the crafting of legislation abolishing public-university DEI programs at the state level. To date, three states—Florida, Texas, and Tennessee—have passed laws abolishing or restricting DEI. A total of 17 states have either passed such laws or are considering them.

Our efforts are bearing fruit. In 2024, the University of Florida, the flagship state institution, announced that it had dissolved its DEI department and terminated the employment of all DEI officials. UF was spending an astonishing $5 million per year on DEI programs, which university president Ben Sasse wisely redirected toward faculty recruitment. The new budget would presumably include recruitment for UF's Hamilton Center, a new home for conservative scholars. Sasse also offered a positive alternative to DEI, promising to hold the institution to the much better standard of "universal human dignity."

Conservatives are rightly celebrating the move as a watershed. DEI is not an inevitability; it is a choice that can be undone.

Giving DEI the Pink Slip

Corporate America is following suit. Firms including Google, Meta, and Zoom have quietly cut back DEI departments and laid off employees. I have recently spoken with a number of Fortune 500 executives, who explained that, following the summer of George Floyd, companies felt immense pressure to "do something" about racial disparities.

But four years later, they have realized that DEI programs undermine productivity, destroy merit-based systems, and poison corporate culture. Because of our successful campaign to expose the true nature of DEI, they now have the political space—in essence, the social permission—to wind down these programs.

But we need to do much more. The best way to conceptualize DEI is as the marriage of ideology and bureaucracy, or, more specifically, as the marriage between critical race theory and affirmative action. On their path to power, DEI activists hijacked the Civil Rights Act of 1964—which, in spirit, enshrines policies of colorblind nondiscrimination—to justify active discrimination against supposed "oppressor" groups. In doing this, they have gained significant leverage.

While the recent firings of DEI employees are a salutary development, the movement to restore colorblind equality can succeed only if we reform civil rights law to reinstate its original focus on individual rights under the law, without regard to race—and dramatically reduce the footprint of critical race ideologies in public universities.

That said, we should celebrate the moment. At the beginning of last year, when we formally launched the "abolish DEI" campaign, it was seen as a fringe, right-wing proposal. Since then, it has achieved significant political victories and become the mainstream position, with widespread support. While momentum is on our side, we should press for maximal demands: abolish DEI in all American institutions, terminate the employment of all DEI bureaucrats, and encourage them to find gainful work elsewhere.

Let us hope that this moment is only the beginning of a "pink slip revolution."

Trump Abolishes DEI for the Feds

Yesterday, President Trump signed an executive order abolishing the "diversity, equity, and inclusion" bureaucracy in the federal government as reported in the Christopher F. Rufo "Trump Abolishes DEI for the Feds" Substack January 2025 post:

The move marks a stunning reversal of fortune from just four years ago, when Black Lives Matter, critical race theory, and DEI seemed unstoppable. Following the death of George Floyd, left-wing race activists made a blitz through America's institutions, rewriting school curricula, altering government policy, and establishing DEI offices in major universities, big-city school districts, and Fortune 100 companies. The Biden administration immediately followed suit, mandating a "whole-of-government equity agenda" that entrenched DEI in the federal government.

No more. President Trump has rescinded the Biden executive order and instructed his Cabinet to "terminate, to the maximum extent allowed by law, all DEI, DEIA, and 'environmental justice' offices and positions," and "all 'equity action plans,' 'equity' actions, initiatives, or programs." In other words, President Trump has signed the death warrant for DEI within the federal government.

The two-year campaign for colorblind equality notches its biggest win yet.

How did we get here? Through patiently building a movement and winning the public debate. At the beginning of 2023, I worked with Florida governor Ron DeSantis to launch the "abolish DEI" campaign. We began by terminating the DEI bureaucracy at New College of Florida, a small public university in Sarasota, where I serve as a trustee. The reaction from the racialist Left was intense. Protesters descended on the campus and the left-wing media published hundreds of articles condemning the move. But we held firm and made the case that public institutions should judge individuals based on their accomplishments, rather than their ancestry.

The argument began to take hold.

The polling data indicated that Americans supported a "colorblind society" over a "race-conscious society" by large margins. Even the New York Times, one of the largest boosters of left-wing racialism, started publishing pieces that criticized DEI. At the same time, the Black Lives Matter movement was ensnared in scandals and the leading intellectual voices of DEI, such as Ibram X. Kendi and Robin DiAngelo, faced sustained public scrutiny and seemed to disappear from the spotlight.

We pushed onward. Governor DeSantis led the way, signing legislation abolishing the DEI bureaucracy in all of Florida's public universities. A dozen other red states followed, restricting DEI programs and banning DEI-style discrimination in their public institutions. The process became a virtuous cycle: each state that passed an anti-DEI bill reduced the risk of the next state doing the same. The campaign moved from the realm of debate to the realm of policy.

Trump's victory over Kamala Harris on November 5 sealed DEI's fate. Corporate America, including companies such as Walmart, and Meta, interpreted the event as an incentive to change, voluntarily terminating their DEI programs before Trump took office. Mark Zuckerberg made it explicit, arguing that the country had reached a "cultural tipping point," which convinced him to stop DEI programs. And Zuckerberg, along with numerous other tech titans, were prominently seated at the inauguration yesterday.

In one way, Trump's executive order yesterday was priced in—people knew it was coming. Still, it is a crowning achievement for those who have built this campaign from the ground up. There will be many fights ahead—the bureaucracy will attempt to evade the order, and more needs doing on civil rights reform in general—but, for the moment, we should celebrate. The forces of left-wing racialism are on the defensive, and the forces of colorblind equality are on the move.

None of it was inevitable—and nothing will be going forward, either. It has taken courage, hard work, and more than a little luck. But this is undoubtedly a moment to feel optimistic. America's institutions are not beyond correction, as many feared. The American people were wise enough to realize that their country might not have survived four or eight more years of government by DEI. They spoke on November 5, and now President Trump is acting accordingly.

Trump Puts Higher Education on Notice for 'Dangerous, Demeaning, and Immoral' DEI Teachings

President Donald Trump's latest executive order seeks to water down diversity, equity and inclusion (DEI) practices in federally funded higher-education institutions in an effort to restore "merit-based opportunity," according to the White House.

During his first two days in office, as reported by Aubrie Spady's "Trump Puts Higher Education on Notice for 'Dangerous, Demeaning, and Immoral' DEI Teachings" Fox News January 2025 story:

Trump issued a slew of executive orders, including ordering that all federal agencies close their DEI offices and put employees in those units on paid leave. To further his effort to deter DEI, the president is launching a federal review of such teachings and practices in educational institutions receiving federal funding.

"Institutions of higher education have adopted and actively use dangerous, demeaning, and immoral race and sex-based preferences under the guise of so-called 'diversity, equity, and inclusion,'" reads the White House order.

The order requires that the attorney general and secretary of education identify potential civil compliance investigations among institutions of higher education with endowments over $1 billion dollars and, accordingly, develop action plans to "deter DEI programs or principles that constitute illegal discrimination or preferences."

Within 120 days, the AG and the secretary of education will issue guidance to state and local educational institutions that receive federal funds or grants or that participate in the student loan program. The focus will be on ensuring compliance with the Supreme Court's decision in *Students for Fair*

Admissions, Inc. v. President and Fellows of Harvard College, a landmark case that held that race-based admissions practices violate the Fourteenth Amendment.

"Illegal DEI and DEIA policies not only violate the text and spirit of our longstanding Federal civil-rights laws, they also undermine our national unity, as they deny, discredit, and undermine the traditional American values of hard work, excellence, and individual achievement in favor of an unlawful, corrosive, and pernicious identity-based spoils system," the memo reads.

The executive order noted that it will not prevent educational institutions or agencies from engaging in "First Amendment-protected" speech.

Social Justice Warriors Crusaded to Mandate DEI in Every Corner of America

Rep. Tim Walberg, R-Mich., who chairs the House Education and the Workforce Committee, applauded Trump for pushing back against the controversial practice.

"For too long, social justice warriors crusaded to mandate DEI in every corner of America. Instead of merit, skills and ability, DEI devotees pushed policies that are antithetical to American exceptionalism," Walberg said. "From the classroom to the boardroom, Americans have felt the negative effects. DEI has bloated education budgets while telling students what to think instead of how to think."

Jonathan Turley, a Fox News contributor and the Shapiro Professor of Public Interest Law at George Washington University, suggested in an analysis of the executive order that it "will send a shock wave through higher education and the resulting agency actions are likely to trigger a tsunami of lawsuits.

Meanwhile, one education expert suggested that universities could begin to pre-comply with new DEI measures.

"It seems very plausible that higher-education institutions will pre-comply, even before the Department of Education or the National Science Foundation writes it into specific projects," Eboo Patel, founder and president of Interfaith America, told the *Chronicle of Higher Education*. "Universities will adopt the spirit of the executive order."

DOGE Slashes Over $100M in DEI Funding at Education Department: 'Win for Every Student'

As reported in the Aubrie Spady Fox News February 2025 article "DOGE Slashes Over $100M in DEI Funding at Education Department: 'Win for Every Student'":

The Department of Education (DOE) is canceling more than $100 million in grants to fund diversity, equity, and inclusion (DEI) training as part of the Department of Government Efficiency (DOGE) sweep of "wasteful" spending.

DOGE, the department led by Elon Musk to cut costs within the federal government, announced the termination of 89 DOE contracts totaling $881 million in a post on X.

Of the nearly $1 billion, DOGE identified $101 million that was being used for DEI training, including teaching educators to "help students understand/interrogate the complex histories involved in oppression, and help students recognize areas of privilege and power on an individual and collective basis."

"Your tax dollars were spent on this," Musk wrote of the DOE spending.

According to DOGE, the education department spent another $1.5 million on a contractor to "observe mailing and clerical operations" at a mail center, which was also terminated in the recent spending sweep.

"DEI was never about 'equity'—it was about enforcing ideological conformity and institutionalizing discrimination. Shutting down these wasteful, divisive programs is a win for every student," Nicki Neily, founder and president of Parents Defending Education, said in response to the spending cut.

"More states need to follow suit," Neily said.

Erika Donalds, wife of Republican Rep. Byron Donalds of Florida, also wrote in response that "the kids can't read" while one program reportedly told educators to 'help students recognize areas of privilege and power'.

DOGE has been leading efforts to vacuum spending within the DOE, announcing in early February the termination of three grants including one funding an institution that had reportedly "previously hosted faculty workshops entitled 'Decolonizing the Curriculum.'"

In his first slew of executive orders, President Donald Trump launched a federal review of DEI teachings and practices in educational institutions receiving federal funding.

Former Education Department press secretary Angela Morabito discusses President Donald Trump's plans to eliminate the Department of Education on 'Fox News Live.'

You Now Have Permission to Stop Pretending

On January 14, 2025, Mark Zuckerberg, the CEO of Meta, formerly Facebook, made a stunning announcement. He was abolishing the company's DEI programs and discontinuing its relationship with fact-checking organizations, which he admitted had become a form of "censorship."

Per the Christopher F. Rufo "You Now Have Permission to Stop Pretending" Substack January 2025 post: The left-wing media immediately attacked the decision, accused him of embracing the MAGA agenda, and predicted a dangerous rise in so-called disinformation.

Zuckerberg's move was carefully calculated and impeccably timed. The November elections, he said, felt like "a cultural tipping point towards once again prioritizing speech." DEI initiatives, especially those related to immigration and gender, had become "disconnected from mainstream conversation"—and untenable.

This is no small about-face. Just four years ago, Zuckerberg spent hundreds of millions of dollars funding left-wing election programs; his role was widely resented by conservatives. And Meta had been at the forefront of any identity-based or left-wing ideological cause.

Why Meta's decision to abolish DEI might be a turning point

Not anymore. As part of the rollout for the announcement, Zuckerberg released a video and appeared on the Joe Rogan podcast, which now functions as a confessional for American elites who no longer believe in left-wing orthodoxies. On the podcast, Zuckerberg sounded less like a California progressive than a right-winger, arguing that the culture needed a better balance of "masculine" and "feminine" energies.

Executives at Meta quickly implemented the new policy, issuing pink slips to DEI employees and moving the company's content-moderation team from California to Texas, in order, in Zuckerberg's words, to "help alleviate concerns that biased employees are excessively censoring content."

Zuckerberg was not the first technology executive to make such an announcement, but he is perhaps the most significant. Facebook is one of the largest firms in Silicon Valley and, with Zuckerberg setting the precedent, many smaller companies will likely follow suit.

The most important signal emanating from this decision is not about a particular shift in policy, however, but a general shift in culture. Zuckerberg has never really been an ideologue. He appears more interested in building his company and staying in the good graces of elite society. But like many successful, self-respecting men, he is also independent-minded and has clearly chafed at the cultural constraints DEI placed on his company. So he seized the moment, correctly sensing that the impending inauguration of Donald Trump reduced the risk and increased the payoff of such a change.

Zuckerberg is certainly not a courageous truth-teller. He assented to DEI over the last decade because that was where the elite status signals were pointing. Now, those signals have reversed, like a barometer suddenly dropping, and he is changing course with them and attempting to shift the blame to the outgoing Biden administration, which, he told Rogan, pressured him to implement censorship—a convenient excuse at an even more convenient moment.

But the good news is that, whatever post hoc rationalizations executives might use, DEI and its cultural assumptions suddenly have run into serious resistance. We may be entering a crucial period in which people feel confident enough to express their true beliefs about DEI, which is antithetical to excellence, and stop pretending that they believe in the cultish ideology of "systemic racism" and race-based guilt.

DEI remains deeply embedded in public institutions, of course, but private institutions and corporations have more flexibility and can dispatch with such programs with the stroke of a pen. Zuckerberg has revealed what this might look like at one of the largest companies. Conservatives can commend him for his decision, while remaining wary. "Trust but verify," as Ronald Reagan used to say, is a good policy all around.

The 45 Companies on the MAGA Anti-DEI Hit List

For President Donald Trump's operatives seeking corporate targets to investigate for "illegal DEI," conservative activists have already done the legwork and drawn up a list according to the Jeff Green and Bloomberg "The 45 Companies on the MAGA Anti-DEI Hit List" article in *Fortune* in February 2025. Source: America First Legal (AFL) and American Alliance for Equal Rights (AAER):

From Amazon.com Inc. to Yum! Brands Inc., 45 companies with a combined market value of almost $10 trillion have been attacked for their DEI efforts in the past three years by groups led by Stephen Miller, now the White House deputy chief of staff for policy, and anti-affirmative action activist Edward Blum. Corporate lawyers and advisers are now poring over the list for clues as to which companies may eventually end up being investigated by the government.

Corporate diversity, equity and inclusion efforts, many of which were implemented less than five years ago when companies rushed to address historic inequities after the murder of George Floyd by a White police officer, are now in sharp focus as the new administration moves to dismantle DEI. The Justice Department, which is preparing a report by March 1, 2025, identifying steps to deter the use of "discriminatory" DEI programs in the private sector, has even threatened criminal investigations.

The department didn't respond to requests for comment on its plans. One of Trump's initial orders regarding DEI asked agency heads to identify up to nine companies or other entitities that might be practicing "illegal DEI."

The order stated that DEI policies aimed at boosting underrepresented groups can violate federal civil-rights laws.

'Target-Rich'

Companies spotlighted in recent lawsuits and complaints are a good indication of "who they're going to go after," said Michael Elkins, who represents businesses on employment law issues as founder and partner at MLE Law in Fort Lauderdale, Florida. "They have a blueprint."

Miller and Blum's groups highlighted what they described as "unlawful" practices at the 45 companies, including hiring based on gender or race, scholarships based on race, and funding for startups owned by underrepresented groups.

"This is a target-rich environment," said Blum, whose lawsuits helped convince the US Supreme Court to end affirmative action in college admissions in 2023 and supercharged right-leaning groups' assault on DEI in corporate America. Companies are exposing themselves to risk by keeping their DEI programs, he said.

Blum wouldn't discuss whether he had direct conversations with administration officials, but said companies should be "mindful" of this government and end practices that are "actionable in court, and unpopular and polarizing." He is pursuing companies including American Airlines Group Inc. and Southwest Airlines Co., and in January 2025, won a settlement with McDonald's Corp.

Lawsuits, Complaints

Anti-DEI activist Robby Starbuck said he's in touch with administration officials and plans to "report any evidence of illegal discrimination against any race or sex we find." Starbuck, who wouldn't give details about his contact with the government, has claimed credit for DEI rollbacks at more than 15 companies, including Walmart Inc., the world's biggest retailer.

Miller's group, America First Legal, has been the most active in its pursuit of company DEI programs that it says discriminates against White men. AFL has filed more than half a dozen lawsuits and more than 30 requests for federal or state investigations of companies.

It says that race, sex and national origin aren't supposed to be "a motivating factor in employment practice," according to Reed Rubinstein, senior vice president at America First Legal. The Trump administration used similar language in a Feb. 5, 2025, memo clarifying instructions to agency heads on how to identify prohibited DEI.

Most of AFL's complaints against DEI practices at companies such as Walt Disney Co., Nike Inc. and IBM Corp. were sent to the US Equal Employment Opportunity Commission, the federal agency that enforces workplace anti-discrimination laws. The companies didn't respond to requests for comment.

DEI Retreat

Already, consulting firms Accenture Plc, Booz Allen Hamilton Holding Corp. and Deloitte have abandoned their diversity goals, citing Trump's executive order banning diversity efforts at federal contractors. Coca-Cola Co. and PepsiCo Inc., both government contractors, said they're preparing to comply with the order.

Companies should be wary of making dramatic changes in DEI policy, even if they have been called out in the past, said Aaron Goldstein, an employment law partner at Dorsey & Whitney's Seattle office. He said he has clients who have been attacked by conservative groups, but wouldn't comment on whether they are on AFL's list.

The Trump administration will likely go after companies that are high profile and have made strong statements in support of DEI in the past, he said. The best a company can do is examine both external and internal communications—and be prepared.

"If you go running from DEI in a very public way, after having embraced it over the last three years, you might be hit by traffic going both ways," Goldstein said. "The worst thing that can happen to a company is: You're still on that list, but you've lost all your good faith and credibility with folks on the other side of these issues."

Companies with outstanding lawsuits:

Company	Complainant	Key Complaint
Ally Financial Inc.	AFL	Hiring based on gender
Amazon.com Inc.	AFL	Race based driver stipend
American Airlines Group Inc.	AAER	Supplier-diversity programs
Bally's Corp.	AAER	Investment based on race
Expedia Group Inc.	AFL	Hiring based on race
IBM Corp.	AFL	Firing based on race
Meta Platforms Inc.	AFL	Hiring based on race and gender
Paramount Global (multiple)	AFL	Hiring/firing based on race
Progressive Corp	AFL	Race based vehicle grants
Southwest Airlines Co.	AAER	Free Flights for Hispanic Students
Target Corp.	AFL	Shareholder risk allegations from DEI

Companies with federal or state complaints made:

Company	Complainant	Key Complaint
Alaska Air Group Inc.	AFL	Hiring based on race
Anheuser-Busch InBev SA/NV	AFL	Hiring based on race and gender
BlackRock Inc.	AFL	Race-based scholarship
Crowdstrike Holdings Inc.	AFL	Promoting based on race
Dick's Sporting Goods Inc.	AFL	Gender discrimination via paid abortion travel
Hasbro Inc.	AFL	Hiring based on race and gender
Hershey Co	AFL	Hiring based on race
Hy-Vee Inc.	AFL	Minority supplier program
Kellanova	AFL	Hiring based on race and gender
Kontoor Brands Inc.	AFL	Hiring based on race
Lyft Inc.	AFL	Gender discrimination via paid abortion travel
Macy's Inc.	AFL	Gender discrimination via paid abortion travel
Major League Baseball	AFL	Race and gender discrimination
Mars Inc.	AFL	Hiring and promoting based on race

Mattel Inc. race	AFL	Hiring and promoting based on
McDonald's Corp.	AFL	Hiring based on race and gender
Microsoft Corp. (Activision)	AFL	Hiring based on race and gender
Morgan Stanley	AFL	Apprenticeship program
NASCAR	AFL	Race and gender discrimination
National Football League	AFL	Rooney Rule is illegal
Nike Inc. race	AFL	Hiring and promoting based on
Nordstrom Inc.	AFL	Hiring based on race and gender
PricewaterhouseCoopers LLP	AFL	Hiring based on race and gender
Salesforce Inc.	AFL	Hiring based on race and gender
Sanofi SA race	AFL	Hiring and promoting based on
Shake Shack Inc.	AFL	Hiring based on race
Smithfield Foods Inc. race	AFL	Hiring and promoting based on
Starbucks Corp.	AFL	Hiring based on race
Twilio Inc.	AFL	Firing based on race
Tyson Foods Inc.	AFL	Hiring based on race
Unilever PLC	AFL	Hiring based on race and gender
Walt Disney Co	AFL	Hiring based on race and gender
Williams-Sonoma Inc.	AFL	Hiring based on race
Yum! Brands Inc.	AFL	Hiring based on race

Appendix

2025 Donald J. Trump Executive Orders – Federal Register:
https://www.federalregister.gov/presidential-documents/executive-orders/donald-trump/2025.

Anti-Wokeness Guidebook Series, Fratire Publishing LLC:
https://www.fratirepublishing.com/anti-wokeness.

Ending Illegal Discrimination and Restoring Merit-Based Opportunity – Executive Order 14173: : https://www.federalregister.gov/documents/2025/01/31/2025-02097/ending-illegal-discrimination-and-restoring-merit-based-opportunity.

Ending Radical and Wasteful Government DEI Programs and Preferencing – Executive Order 14151:
https://www.federalregister.gov/documents/2025/01/29/2025-01953/ending-radical-and-wasteful-government-dei-programs-and-preferencing.

President Donald J. Trump Protects Civil Rights and Merit Based Opportunity by Ending Illegal DEI: https://www.whitehouse.gov.

Reforming the Federal Hiring Process and Restoring Merit to Government Service – Executive Order 14170:
https://www.federalregister.gov/documents/2025/01/30/2025-02094/reforming-the-federal-hiring-process-and-restoring-merit-to-government-service.

Trump's Executive Orders on Diversity, Equity, and Inclusion, Explained:
https://civilrights.org/resource/anti-deia-eos/.

Winning School Board Elections With an Anti-Wokeness Platform:
https://www.fratirepublishing.com/anti-wokeness/winning-school-board-elections.

Woke Free Campus Guide for Students, Faculty and Alumni:
https://www.fratirepublishing.com/anti-wokeness/woke-free-campus-guide.

References

Anderson, Kevin. "DEI or MEI: Which Builds Better Teams?" Energy Central. July 11, 2024. https://energycentral.com/c/hr/dei-or-mei-which-builds-better-teams.

Beran, Michael Knox. "Beyond Woke—a Return to Lincoln?" *City Journal.* July 4, 2022. https://www.city-journal.org/american-birthright-a-new-model-of-social-studies.

Callaham, Sheila. "Does SHRM'S Removal Of 'Equity' From Inclusion, Equity And Diversity Point To A New Strategy Or Signal Something Much Bigger?" *Forbes.* July 28, 2024. https://www.forbes.com/sites/sheilacallaham/2024/07/28/does-shrms-removal-of-equity-from-inclusion-equity-and-diversity-point-to-a-new-strategy-or-signal-something-much-bigger/.

Cloud, Michael (TX-27) and Eric Schmitt (R-MO). Press. February 04, 2025. https://cloud.house.gov/posts/release-cloud-and-schmitt-introduce-bill-to-codify-into-law-trumps-agenda-ending-dei-in-federal-government.

de Varna, Vic Porak. "Moving from DEI to MEI: An Alternative Approach for Enhancing Workforce Performance." LinkedIn. October 2, 2024. https://www.linkedin.com/pulse/moving-from-dei-mei-alternative-approach-enhancing-porak-de-varna-w6coe/?trackingId=ldt67chERv6WqVmfJwc%2F5w%3D%3D.

Dreher, Rod. "DEI Training: Harmful, Phony, And Expensive." The American Conservative. Jan. 17, 2023. https://www.theamericanconservative.com/dei-training-harmful-phony-and-expensive/.

Ellis, Nicquel Terry. "What is DEI, and why is it dividing America?" CNN. January 23, 2025. https://www.cnn.com/2025/01/22/us/dei-diversity-equity-inclusion-explained.

Executive Order: Ending Radical and Wasteful Government DEI Programs and Preferencing. White House. January 20, 2025. https://www.whitehouse.gov/presidential-actions/2025/01/ending-radical-and-wasteful-government-dei-programs-and-preferencing/.

Graham, Jennifer. "America's 'Great Awokening,' Explained." *Desert News.* March 23, 2021. https://www.deseret.com/indepth/2021/3/23/22332164/americas-great-awokening-explained-woke-social-justice-racial-justice/.

Green, Jeff and *Bloomberg.* "The 45 Companies on the MAGA Anti-DEI Hit List." *Fortune.* February 19, 2025. https://fortune.com/2025/02/19/maga-anti-diversity-dei-hit-list-companies-list/.

Gulliver, Katrina. "Cancelling the Cancellers." *City Journal.* Oct. 13, 2023. https://www.city-journal.org/article/cancelling-the-cancellers.

Haidt, Jonathan and Greg Lukianoff. "How To Keep Your Corporation Out of the Culture War." Persuasion. Dec. 3, 2021. https://www.persuasion.community/p/haidt-and-lukianoff-how-to-end-corporate.

Hankinson, Simon. "How Discriminatory DEI Ideology Replicates Itself in the Federal Bureaucracy." The Heritage Foundation. Oct. 17, 2023. https://www.heritage.org/progressivism/commentary/how-discriminatory-dei-ideology-replicates-itself-the-federal-bureaucracy.

Hanson, Victor Davis. "Wokeness: An Evil of Our Age." Independent Institute. September 13, 2021. https://www.independent.org/news/article.asp?id=13758.

Jourdan, Lee. "7 Metrics to Measure Your Organization's DEI Progress." *Harvard Business Review.* May 4, 2023. https://hbr.org/2023/05/7-metrics-to-measure-your-organizations-dei-progress.

Keis, Ken. "Why MEI Is Superior To DEI: A Case For Merit, Excellence And Intelligence." Brainz Magazine. Sep. 3, 2024. https://www.brainzmagazine.com/post/why-mei-is-superior-to-dei-a-case-for-merit-excellence-and-intelligence.

Kelly, Jack. "President Trump Shifts To 'Merit, Excellence And Intelligence' In The Workplace And Away From DEI." Forbes. Feb. 1, 2025. https://www.forbes.com/sites/jackkelly/2025/02/01/president-trump-shifts-to-merit-excellence-and-intelligence-in-the-workplace-and-away-from-dei/.

Maranto, Robert and Michael Mills, Catherine Salmon. "What do we really mean by 'diversity, equity and inclusion'?" *The Hill.* November 8, 2024. https://thehill.com/opinion/education/3718803-what-do-we-really-mean-by-diversity-equity-and-inclusion/.

McGuire, Steven. "How One College Spends More Than $30M on 241 DEI Staffers … and the Damage it Does to Kids." *New York Post.* Jan. 11, 2024.

https://nypost.com/2024/01/11/opinion/dei-boondoggle-costs-us-millions-and-harms-students-it-claims-to-help/.

Miller, Wade and Dan Morenoff, Ilya Shapiro, David E. Bernstein, James Sherk, Judge Glock, Christopher F. Rufo. "How to Defeat Left-Wing Racialism." *City Journal.* Summer 2023. https://www.city-journal.org/article/how-to-defeat-left-wing-racialism.

Minkin, Rachel. "Views of DEI Have Become Slightly More Negative Among U.S. Workers." Pew Research Center. Nov. 19, 2024. https://www.pewresearch.org/short-reads/2024/11/19/views-of-dei-have-become-slightly-more-negative-among-us-workers/.

Rufo, Christopher F. "A New Civil Rights Agenda." *City Journal.* Jan. 17 2024. https://www.city-journal.org/article/a-new-civil-rights-agenda.

Rufo, Christopher F. "Giving DEI the Pink Slip." *City Journal.* Mar. 04 2024. https://www.city-journal.org/article/giving-dei-the-pink-slip.

Rufo, Christopher F. "Trump Abolishes DEI for the Feds." Substack. Jan. 21, 2025. https://substack.com/home/post/p-155346530?source=queue.

Rufo, Christopher F. "You Now Have Permission to Stop Pretending." Substack. Jan. 14, 2025. https://christopherrufo.com/p/you-now-have-permission-to-stop-pretending.

Spady, Aubrie. "DOGE Slashes Over $100M in DEI Funding at Education Department: 'Win for Every Student'." Fox News. February 11, 2025 https://www.foxnews.com/politics/doge-slashes-over-100m-dei-funding-education-department-win-every-student.

Spady, Aubrie. "Trump Puts Higher Education on Notice for 'Dangerous, Demeaning, and Immoral' DEI Teachings." Fox News. January 22, 2025. https://www.foxnews.com/politics/trump-puts-higher-education-notice-dangerous-demeaning-immoral-dei-teachings.

Taylor, Adelaide. "Merit vs. Diversity: The Debate Surrounding MEI and DEI Hiring Principles." B2B Daily. June 28, 2024. https://b2bdaily.com/hrtech/merit-vs-diversity-the-debate-surrounding-mei-and-dei-hiring-principles/.

Weech, Edward. "Sowell's Summary Argument." The Russell Kirk Center. May 26, 2024. https://kirkcenter.org/reviews/sowells-summary-argument/.

Wood, Alan. "DEI Exposed: The Dangers of Forced Conformity in Diversity Equity & Inclusion." Global Watchdog. March 13, 2024. https://gwmac.com/dei-exposed-forced-conformity/.

Yoshino, Kenji and David Glasgow. "DEI Is Under Attack. Here's How Companies Can Mitigate the Legal Risks." *Harvard Business Review*. January 05, 2024. https://hbr.org/2024/01/dei-is-under-attack-heres-how-companies-can-mitigate-the-legal-risks.

Index

E

Author Bio

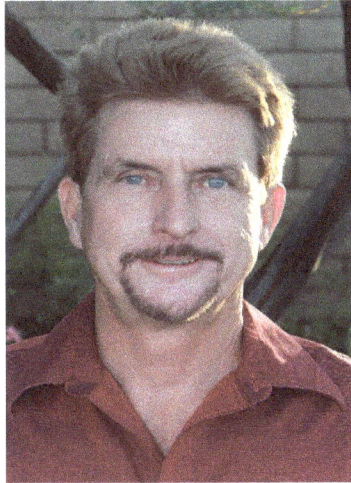

Corey Lee Wilson

Corey Lee Wilson was raised an atheist by his liberal *Playboy* Bunny mother, has three Anglo-Hispanic siblings, a bi-racial daughter, a brother who died of AIDS, baptized a Protestant by his conservative grandparents, attended temple with his Jewish foster parents, baptized again as a Catholic for his first Filipina wife, attends Buddhist ceremonies with his second Thai wife, became an agnostic on his own free will for most of his life, and is a lifetime independent voter.

Corey felt the sting of intellectual humility by repeating the 4th grade and attended eighteen different schools (17 in California and one in the Bahamas) before putting himself through college (without parents) at Mt. San Antonio College and Cal Poly Pomona University (while on triple secret probation).

Named Who's Who of American College Students in 1984, he received a BS in Economics (summa cum laude) and won his fraternity's most prestigious undergraduate honor, the Phi Kappa Tau Fraternity's Shideler Award, both in 1985. In 2020, he became a member of the Heterodox Academy, in 2021 a member of the National Association of Scholars and 1776 Unites, and in 2023 became a member of Moms for Liberty.

As a satirist and fraternity man, Corey started Fratire Publishing in 2012 and transformed the fiction "fratire" genre to a respectable and viewpoint diverse non-fiction genre promoting practical knowledge and wisdom to help everyday people navigate safely through the many hazards of life. In 2019, he founded the S.A.P.I.E.N.T. Being to help promote freedom of speech, viewpoint diversity, intellectual humility and most importantly advance sapience in America's students and campuses.

Some readers might be prone to ask why would someone raised as a wild-hippy-gypsy child of the Sixties take the conservative path and champion conservative causes?

Quick answer: In this day and age it's the reasonable, logical, and sapient thing to do. By comparison, there is nothing "sapient" about the Progressivism movement and the woke madness that follows it throughout our educational, governmental, and business systems.

Furthermore, to quote Ronald Reagan, "There's a flickering spark in us all which, if struck at just the right age, can light the rest of our lives." His spark was ignited in college when he experienced first-hand in the early Eighties the growing illiberalism at his college newspaper and its persistent bias against conservatives, Christians, and President Reagan.

Hopefully, this *Woke Free Work Places* guide will do the same to spark your inspiration and help you craft your anti-wokeness platform for your organization's well-being.

www.ingramcontent.com/pod-product-compliance
Lightning Source LLC
Chambersburg PA
CBHW042332030426
42335CB00027B/3312